Write it Down!

A GUIDED JOURNAL
OF IDEAS, STRATEGIES,
AND REFLECTIONS FOR
BEGINNING TEACHERS

Dawn L. Kolakoski, Ed.D.
Hudson Valley Community College

THOMSON

DELMAR LEARNING

Australia   Canada   Mexico   Singapore   Spain   United Kingdom   United States

THOMSON

DELMAR LEARNING

Write it Down!
A Guided Journal of Ideas, Strategies, and Reflections for Beginning Teachers
Dawn L. Kolakoski, Ed.D.

**Vice President,
Career Education SBU:**
Dawn Gerrain

Director of Editorial:
Sherry Gomoll

Acquisitions Editor:
Erin O'Connor

Editorial Assistant:
Ivy Ip

Director of Production:
Wendy A. Troeger

Production Editor:
Joy Kocsis

Director of Marketing:
Donna J. Lewis

Channel Manager:
Nigar Hale

Cover Design:
Dutton & Sherman

Composition:
Stratford Publishing Services

For permission to use material from this text or product, contact us at
Tel   (800) 730-2214
Fax   (800) 730-2215
www.thomsonrights.com

Library of Congress Cataloging-in-Publication Data

Kolakoski, Dawn L.
    Write it down! : a guided journal of ideas, strategies, and reflections for beginning teachers / Dawn L. Kolakoski.—1st ed.
        p. cm.
    Includes index.
    ISBN 1-4018-4064-7
    1. First-year teachers—Handbooks, manuals, etc.
    2. Student teachers—Handbooks, manuals, etc. 3. Early childhood education—Handbooks, manuals, etc. I. Title.

LB2844.1.N4K65 2004
371.1—dc21   2003014446

Contents

Preface   ix
Acknowledgments   xi
Introduction: A Letter to the Student   xiii

PART I JOURNAL OF IDEAS 1

CHAPTER 1
JOURNAL OF IDEAS: ART 3

Creative Art Activities 4
Art Projects 5
Art-Materials Recipes 6
Supplies: Where Did They Get That? 7
Art-Materials Supply List 8
Ideas for Displaying Children's Artwork 9
Children's Literature: Art 10
Teacher Resource Books: Art 11
Safety Issues to Remember 12

CHAPTER 2
JOURNAL OF IDEAS: MUSIC AND MOVEMENT 13

Favorite Fingerplays 14
Songs Enjoyed by Children 15
Successful Creative Movement Activities 16
Movement with Props (Hoops, Scarves, Bean Bags) 17
Recordings to Note 18
Music Interest Centers 19
Using Instruments with Children 20
Children's Literature: Music 21
Teacher Resource Books: Music and Movement 22

CHAPTER 3
JOURNAL OF IDEAS: LANGUAGE ARTS 23

Creative Drama 24
Children's Literature: Language Arts 25
Emergent Literacy in Early Childhood Settings 26
Poetry: Creative Activities 27
Favorite Poems 28
Alphabet: Effective Teaching Strategies K–2 29
Spelling and Word Games 30
Sight Words and Word-Wall Ideas 31
Writing Activities 32
Author Studies 33
Teacher Resource Books: Language Arts 34
Ideas and Advice about Teaching Reading K–2 35

CHAPTER 4
JOURNAL OF IDEAS: SOCIAL STUDIES 36

Self and Family: Activities/Centers 37
Cultural Activities 38
Developmentally Appropriate Holiday Activities 39
Home and Community: Activities/Centers 40
Field Trips 41
Guest Speakers/Class Visitors 42
Dramatic Play Prop Boxes 43
Geography and Mapping 44
Teaching Historical Events 45
Children's Literature: Social Studies Concepts 46
Teacher Resource Books: Social Studies 47

CHAPTER 5
JOURNAL OF IDEAS: SCIENCE 48

Discovery Centers 49
Water Table Ideas 50
Investigations 51
Experiments 52
Nature Activities 53
Recipes for Science Materials 54
Class Pets 55
Invention Centers 56
Children's Literature: Science Concepts 57
Science Projects and Science Fair Ideas 58
The Scientific Method 59
Science Materials to Find or Purchase 60
Technology in the Classroom 61
Computer Software to Note 62
Teacher Resource Books: Science 63

CHAPTER 6
JOURNAL OF IDEAS: COOKING AND NUTRITION 64

"One-Cup" Cooking Ideas. 65
Whole-Group Cooking Ideas. 67
Nutrition Activities 69
Healthy Snacks 70
Children's Literature: Cooking and Nutrition 71
Cookbooks for Children 72
Teacher Resource Books: Cooking and Nutrition 73

CHAPTER 7
JOURNAL OF IDEAS: MATH 74

Counting, Cardinal Numbers, and Numerals. 75
Ordinal Numbers (First, Second, Third . . .) 76
Shape and Form 77
Classification and Seriation (Order) Activities 78
Size and Measurement. 79
Patterning. 80
Block Play. 81
Graphing Activities. 82
Money Concepts 83
Calendar Activities and Routines for K–2. 84
1th Day of School Activities 85
Telling Time 86
Adding and Subtracting. 87
Place Value 88
Math Games and Materials 89
Children's Literature: Math Concepts. 90
Teacher Resource Books: Math 91

CHAPTER 8
JOURNAL OF IDEAS: MOTOR DEVELOPMENT. 92

Fine Motor Activities 93
Fine Motor Development: Writing 94
Gross Motor Activities and Games. 95
Playground Play. 96
Outdoor Water Play. 97
Outdoor Sandbox Play 98
Outdoor Play Equipment 99
Teacher Resource Books: Motor Development. 100

CHAPTER 9
JOURNAL OF IDEAS: INTEGRATED CURRICULUM . . . 101

Concept Web Example. 102
Concept Web Forms. 103
Theme or Unit Example 104
Theme or Unit Form 105
Project Approach. 106
Teacher Resource Books: Themes, Units, and Projects 107

CHAPTER 10
JOURNAL OF IDEAS: OBSERVATION AND ASSESSMENT 108

Observation Methods 109
Case Study 110

CHAPTER 11
JOURNAL OF IDEAS: HEALTH AND SAFETY 111

Health and Safety Activities 112
Fire Safety 113
Emergency Procedures 114
Procedures for Keeping Children Safe and Healthy 115
Common Childhood Illnesses and Allergies 116
Basic First Aid and Infant/Child CPR: Notes 117
Children's Literature: Health and Safety Concepts 118
Teacher Resource Books: Health and Safety 119

CHAPTER 12
JOURNAL OF IDEAS: INFANTS AND TODDLERS 120

Infant Care 121
Attachment between Caregiver and Child 122
Sensory Activities for Infants 123
Motor Activities for Infants 124
Music Activities for Infants 125
Language Activities for Infants 126
Lullabies and Other Recordings for Babies 127
Equipment and Toys for Infants 128
Toddler Care 129
Toddler Behavior 130
Toddler Activities, Songs, and Games 131
Books for Infants and Toddlers 132
Equipment and Toys for Toddlers 133
Teacher Resource Books: Infants and Toddlers 134
Communicating with Parents 135

CHAPTER 13
JOURNAL OF IDEAS: BEHAVIOR STRATEGIES 136

Indirect Guidance Strategies 137
Successful Room Arrangements 138
Direct Guidance Strategies 139
Early Childhood Transition Strategies 140
Early Childhood Mealtime Strategies 141
Early Childhood Group-Time Strategies 142
Elementary Classroom-Management Strategies 143
Attention Getters 144

Elementary Class Motivators. 145
Elementary Transition Strategies. 146
Walking in the Halls. 147
Conflict-Management Strategies 148
Calming Upset Children 149
Teacher Resource Books: Behavior Strategies. 150

CHAPTER 14
JOURNAL OF IDEAS: WORKING WITH CHILDREN WITH SPECIAL NEEDS. 151

Behavior Strategies for Children with Special Needs 152
IEPs—Individualized Education Plans 153
Modification of Materials. 154
Adaptation of Teaching Methods 155
Modifications of Room Arrangements 156
Sign Language. 157
Differentiated Instruction 158
Assessment. 159
Children's Literature: Special Needs 160
Teacher Resource Books: Special Needs. 161

CHAPTER 15
JOURNAL OF IDEAS: TEACHING MATERIALS 162

Bulletin-Board Ideas 163
Teaching Charts. 164
Interactive Bulletin Boards 165
Felt-Board Props 166
Puppets 167
Teacher-Made Instruments. 168
Motivating Props 169
Management Props: Pictorial Schedules 170
Management Props: Attendance Charts 171
Management Props: Job Boards 172
Management Props: Choice Boards. 173
Teacher Resource Books: Teaching Materials 174
Web Sites for Teachers 175

CHAPTER 16
JOURNAL OF IDEAS: WORKING WITH PARENTS. . . . 176

Parent Communications. 177
Parent-Teacher Conferences. 178
Problem Solving with Parents 179
Open-House Ideas 180
Progress Reports. 181
Special Events for Families 182
Parents as Volunteers 183

PART II JOURNAL OF REFLECTION 185

CHAPTER 17
JOURNAL OF REFLECTION: BECOMING A REFLECTIVE TEACHER 187
What Is Reflection? 187
Steps to Becoming Reflective 187
How to Complete a Reflective Entry 188
Becoming Reflective: An Example 189
Becoming Reflective: Journal Page 191

CHAPTER 18
JOURNAL OF REFLECTION 193
Journal Pages 194

CHAPTER 19
JOURNAL OF REFLECTION: DEVELOPING A TEACHING PHILOSOPHY 204
Reflection Pages: Developing My Teaching Philosophy 205
Reflection Pages: My Best Activities, Lessons, and/or Centers 211
Reflection Pages: Thoughts about Children 212
Reflection Pages: My Teaching 213
Reflection Pages: Goals 220
Reflection Pages: Notes of Conferences with Cooperating Teacher, Supervisor, or Mentor 222

CHAPTER 20
JOURNAL OF REFLECTION: PROFESSIONAL DEVELOPMENT 223
Reflection Pages: School Structure 224
Reflection Pages: Faculty/Staff Meetings 225
Reflection Pages: Committee Meetings 226
Reflection Pages: Communications 227
Reflection Pages: Ethical Issues 228
Reflection Pages: Advocacy—Volunteer Work 229
Reflection Pages: Videography 230
Reflection Pages: Courses Completed 231
Reflection Pages: Conferences and Seminars Attended 232
Reflection Pages: Professional Organization Membership(s) 233
Reflection Pages: References I Can Use When Applying for a Position 234
Reflection Pages: Goals—Professional Development Plans 235
Reflection Pages: Certificates and Degrees Earned 236
Reflection Pages: Honors and Awards 237

Index   239

Preface

This book is designed as a reflection journal for early childhood and/or elementary education student teachers who are either observing or interning in early childhood (birth to grade 3) settings. During these experiences, students will have many opportunities to observe successful teaching practices being implemented by their cooperating teachers, assistants, special subject teachers, and other specialists. The intent of this book is to help focus the student on observing and recording developmentally appropriate curriculum practices, as well as to reflect on their own development as a teacher. The book is intended to serve as a supplement to the many curriculum texts already on the market.

This book has been perforated and three-hole punched so pages can be easily removed and placed in a binder for you to add pages if additional space is needed for journal entires. Additional blank forms may be downloaded from the *Online Resource™ to Accompany Write It Down! A Guided Journal of Ideas, Strategies, and Reflections.* You can access these forms at http://www.earlychilded.delmar.com

The book is divided into two sections. The first section, termed a "journal of ideas," provides spaces to record a variety of curriculum ideas in art, music, movement, science, social studies, mathematics, language arts, cooking, motor development, and integrated curriculum. It also includes chapters for developmentally appropriate teaching props and bulletin boards, observation and assessment methods, behavior strategies, health and safety, working with infants and toddlers, working with children with special needs, communicating with parents, and teaching resources. Each page includes an example of an observed activity to serve as a starting point for the students' own observations. Caution should be exercised when implementing any of the suggested activities.

The second section, termed a "journal of reflection," has been designed as a space for the students to reflect on their own teaching experiences. Recommendations of the National Board for Professional Teaching Standards (1996) describe reflective practice as "central to teachers' responsibilities as professionals to steadily extend their knowledge, perfect their teaching, and refine their evolving philosophy of education" (p. 93). In this section, an explanation of reflection and its value to teachers is followed by areas to record successes and failures. Each section is guided to help students focus on their own strengths and weaknesses, as well as future goals.

One chapter has space to record weekly reflections for a semester. The final chapter summarizes the student teaching experience and includes spaces to record goals and professional development plans.

Research shows that beginning teachers struggle in their first years with planning and curriculum development. This book can serve as a personal curriculum guide for students as they begin their careers. Students will no doubt value a book they have written themselves—filled with ideas and strategies that they know to be successful. This book has been designed to be used as a supplementary text to any course that includes a field observation, including methods and materials courses, curriculum courses, foundations or introductory courses, practicum seminars, courses on developmentally appropriate practices, and student teaching or interning experiences. It may also be a helpful resource to practitioners in the field who wish to record their own teaching strategies.

NAEYC (1996). National Board for Professional Teaching Standards, in *Guidelines for Preparation of Early Childhood Professionals*. Washington, DC: NAEYC.

Acknowledgments

Designing and writing a book (even a supplementary one) takes much time and patience, especially from family members! I wish to thank my two daughters, Kate and Becky, for giving me their support and, more importantly, the time to work on this project. I also wish to thank the following student teachers who did a "test run" with the draft and provided helpful suggestions for improvements: Jessica Glynn, Debbie Kearsing, Jackie Robitaille, Jessica Valcik, April Whitbeck, Sally Tedesco, Lisa Quail, Jessica Guild, and Erin Martinelli.

Many of the examples found in this book come from years of supervising student teachers in the field. Thanks to the many cooperating teachers and student teachers who shared their ideas with me and my students:

Robin Applebee, First-Grade Teacher, Clarksville Elementary School, Clarksville, NY
Anne Bacher, Kindergarten Teacher, Slingerlands Elementary School, Slingerlands, NY
Karen Barrett, Kindergarten Teacher, Okte Elementary School, Clifton Park, NY
Joanne Bennet, Preschool Teacher, The Parker School, Averill Park, NY
Mary Blanchard, Kindergarten Teacher, Milton Terrace Elementary School, Ballston Spa, NY
Margaret Dilgen, Kindergarten Teacher, Glenmont Elementary School, Glenmont, NY
Val Falco, Third-Grade Teacher, Glenmont Elementary School, Glenmont, NY
Kim Ganley, Second-Grade Teacher, Glenmont Elementary School, Glenmont, NY
Claudia Hauser, First-Grade Teacher, Milton Terrace Elementary School, Ballston Spa, NY
Debbie Kearsing, Student Teacher, Pals Child Care Center, Clifton Park, NY
Claire Kohler, Preschool Teacher, Shenendehowa Methodist Preschool, Clifton Park, NY
Deanie McCarthy, Second-Grade Teacher, Milton Terrace Elementary School, Ballston Spa, NY
Sharon Meeker, Preschool Teacher, Albany Head Start, Albany, NY
Tiffany Millious, Student Teacher, Clarksville Elementary School, Clarksville, NY
Sue Pagoda, Toddler Teacher, Albany Jewish Community Center, Albany, NY
Nancy Pope, Second-Grade Teacher, Stevens Elementary School, Burnt Hills, NY
Sarah Schmitt, Occupational Therapist, Guilderland Central Schools, Guilderland, NY
April Whitbeck, Student Teacher, Clarksville Elementary School, Clarksville, NY
Audrey Woliner, First-Grade Teacher, Stevens Elementary School, Burnt Hills, NY

Appreciation also goes to my colleagues at Hudson Valley Community College for their never-ending support: Dr. Joan Lawson; Dr. Rita Egan; Eileen Mahoney; Diana Pane; my "suite-mate,"

Nancy Cupolo, who gave me valuable ideas to add for working with children with special needs; and to Tim Graves, who reviewed the chapter on Infants and Toddlers. I also wish to thank my friend Dr. Michelle Gillis for her helpful ideas for Chapter 14.

I would also like to thank the following reviewers, enlisted by Delmar Learning, for their helpful suggestions and constructive criticism:

Julie Bakerlis
Quinsigamond Community College
Worcester, MA

Audrey Beard, Ed.D.
Albany State University
Albany, GA

Alice Beyrent
Hesser College
Manchester, NH

Sylvia Brooks, Ed.D.
University of Delaware
Newark, DE

Mary Lou Brotherson, Ed.D.
Barry University
Miami, FL

Pamela Davis, Ph.D.
Henderson State University
Arkadelphia, AR

Judy Lindman
Rochester Community and Technical College
Rochester, MN

Ruth Sasso
Naugatuck Valley Community-Technical College
Waterbury, CT

Introduction:
A Letter to the Student

Dear Student,

This journal is designed for you, the student who is observing or student teaching in an early childhood or elementary setting. During these experiences, you will have many opportunities to observe other teachers implementing successful activities, lessons, or units. You will see many bulletin boards or other types of displays that are impressive. You will see teachers helping children make the transition from activity to activity with little effort, behavior strategies that work well, and field trips to remember.

At the time, you think you will remember everything that you see. In reality, however, by the time you start teaching in your own classroom, these ideas will be but fleeting thoughts. Research on beginning teachers shows that most struggle to develop their own strategies during that first year. If you had only written it down! This book has been designed to help you complete that task. You will find sections for curriculum ideas, display ideas, field trips, transitions, behavior and guidance techniques, classroom-management ideas, teacher props, and recommended resources.

This book has been perforated and three-hole punched so pages can be easily removed and placed in a binder for you to add pages if additional space is needed for journal entires. Additional blank forms may be downloaded from the Online Resource™ to Accompany Write It Down! A Guided Journal of Ideas, Strategies, and Reflections. You can access these forms at http://www.earlychilded.delmar.com

Your cooperating teacher can be your best resource, but don't exclude ideas from the classroom next door, or a different grade or age level down the hall. Assistant teachers may also have good ideas. Specialists who visit your classroom can give you wonderful ideas for working with children with special needs, so don't forget to record ideas from the speech therapist, physical therapist, occupational therapist, and psychologist. Substitute teachers are also good resources for behavior-management strategies. They have many "tricks" to motivate a less-than-enthusiastic class! All these strategies can work for you when you begin your career.

The second half of the book is for your own reflections. My advice is to be honest. Have goals for yourself and look back often to see how much you have grown.

So pay attention to what you observe while in the field and don't forget to WRITE IT DOWN!

Dawn L. Kolakoski, Ed.D.

PART I

Journal of Ideas·

CHAPTER 1

JOURNAL OF IDEAS
Art

WHO TO OBSERVE:

- Cooperating teachers
- Assistants
- Art teachers
- Art therapists
- Other staff members

IDEA PAGES:

- **Creative Art Activities:** Include painting, printing, crayon art, collage, fiber arts, construction, and any other activities you want to remember. Be sure to list materials used.
- **Art Projects:** Include long-term projects such as making paper, papier-mâché, and group art.
- **Art-Materials Recipes:** How did she make that play dough? Write down all those marvelous recipes for doughs, finger paints, goop, putty, bubbles, papier-mâché, and slime.

- **Supplies:** Where did they get that? Here's a place to record addresses or Web sites for art-supply catalogues. Make a list of art materials that you would like for your own classroom.
- **Art Displays:** Describe how you have seen children's artwork displayed.
- **Children's Books with Art Concepts:** What books have you found to integrate with art?

Creative Art Activities

Observed Activity	Age or Grade Level
Example: Children made their own puffy-paint pictures using a mixture of ½ glue to ½ shaving cream painted on blue paper. When dry, the pictures were puffy and 3-D. The teacher used this activity as a follow-up to the book *It Looked Like Spilt Milk*.	K

Art Projects

Observed Activity	Age or Grade Level
Example: Making Paper This activity took place over several days. *Day 1:* Have the children rip discarded paper into small bits. Put the pieces into a bucket of water. Let it sit for two days. Over the two days, have the children play with the pulp by ripping it apart more in the water. My class really enjoyed doing this. It was very sensory. *Day 3:* Whip the pulp mixture with a wire wisk. Add one tablespoon of corn starch to the mixture. The teacher brought in screens that were wrapped with duct tape around the edges for safety. Have the child dip the screen into the mixture and pull up gently. Put the screen with the pulp on top onto a thick towel. Put a piece of wax paper on top of the pulp and roll a rolling pin or your hands over it to press out the water. Gently peel off the wax paper. Flip over the screen and gently tap the back to have the newly made paper fall off. Put it onto a sheet of paper to dry. *Day 4 or 5:* The paper will be dry and ready to paint, write on, or decorate!	Grades K–2

Art-Materials Recipes

Example: Clean Mud (Ages 4+)

6 rolls of toilet paper
1½ cups of Borax®
2 small bars of Ivory® soap

In a large container, unroll all of the toilet paper and discard the cardboard rolls. Grate the two bars of soap on top of the paper and add the Borax®. Pour in enough water to saturate the toilet paper. Work it all together with your hands into a soapy mixture. (Add water as needed.) Lasts for months.

Supplies: Where Did They Get That?

Company Name	Address	Phone/Web Site	Types of Materials
Example: Discount School Supply	P. O. Box 7636 Spreckels, CA 93962	1–800-627–2829 www.discountschoolsupply.com	Liquid water colors Large coffee filters Paint gadgets Bio-paints

Art-Materials Supply List

Art Supply	Sizes/Colors/Notes	Uses
Example: Liquid water colors	8-ounce bottles, comes in 13 colors. Spray bottles also available.	Great for dip-and-dye coffee filters, direct painting, straw painting, and spray painting on snow!

 Ideas for Displaying Children's Artwork

Display Observed	Age or Grade Level
Example: The children in Mrs. W's class created their own bulletin board about the ocean. They first created the water by dipping paper towels in blue liquid water colors and dabbing them onto a large white piece of paper. Some children used sponges. They created seaweed by painting with pine branches using red, green, and brown paint. Once this was dry, each child placed his or her drawing of an ocean creature onto the board. They were very proud.	Grades K–2

Children's Literature: Art

Title	Author	Publisher/Date/ISBN	Age or Grade Level	Art Concepts
Example: *A Rainbow All Around Me*	Sandra L. Pinkney	Cartwheel Books 2002 ISBN: 043930928X	Preschool	Colors—the book has colorful photographs of children creating art and representing all of the colors.
Example: *Katie Meets the Impressionists*	James Mayhew	The Watts Publishing Group 1998 ISBN: 1860397689	Grades 1–3	Katie visits a museum and is magically transported into a Monet painting!

 Teacher Resource Books: Art

Title	Author	Publisher/Date/ISBN	Age or Grade Level	Notes
Example: *Preschool Art: It's the Process Not the Product*	MaryAnn Kohl	Gryphon House 1994 ISBN: 0876591683	Preschool–elementary	Includes hundreds of creative art activities. Each page lists materials needed, the art process, and variations.

Safety Issues to Remember

Type of Material or Concern	Observation or Advice
Example: Powdered (dry) tempera paints	The presenter of an art workshop for teachers noted that powdered tempera paint should never be used by children. She suggested that teachers avoid activities that call for children to work directly with the powder. Inhalation of the dust can cause respiratory distress and even death in children who are asthmatic. She recommends liquid tempera or water colors as a safer alternative.

CHAPTER 2

JOURNAL OF IDEAS
Music and Movement

WHO TO OBSERVE:

- Cooperating teachers
- Assistants
- Music teachers and therapists
- Other staff members
- Guest artists/visitors

IDEA PAGES:

- **Favorite Finger Plays:** Be sure to include hand motions and any props used, such as glove puppets, finger puppets, and felt-board pieces.
- **Favorite Songs:** Record the words and tune (if you know it!).
- **Creative Movement Activities:** Include movement, games, and dances.
- **Movement with Props:** Props such as parachutes, hoops, bean bags, and scarves motivate children to participate. How have you seen these used?

- **Recordings to Note:** What was that great Hap Palmer song all the children loved? Make note of popular recordings and related activities.
- **Music Interest Centers:** Describe "sound boxes" or musical centers you have seen or designed.
- **Using Instruments with Children:** How have you seen instruments used? With stories? With recordings? With songs?
- **Children's Literature and Teacher Resource Books:** List both children's books and teachers' books that you've seen used with songs or sound stories.

Favorite Fingerplays

Example: *Two Little Blackbirds*

Two little blackbirds sitting on a hill (hide hands behind your back)
One named Jack (bring out RH pointer)
One named Jill (bring out LH pointer)
Fly away Jack (hide RH)
Fly away Jill (hide LH)
Come back Jack (bring back RH pointer)
Come back Jill (bring back LH pointer)

This worked great with blackbird stick puppets! For additional verses, substitute various birds such as sparrows, toucans, or parrots. Also try substituting children's names instead of Jack and Jill.

Songs Enjoyed by Children

Words and Tune	Age or Grade Level
Example: *The Animals on the Farm* (sing to "Wheels on the Bus") The cow on the farm says, "Moo, moo, moo, Moo, moo, moo, moo, moo, moo." The cow on the farm says "moo, moo, moo" All day long.	Ages 2–5

Successful Creative Movement Activities

Movement Activity	Age or Grade Level
Example: Space Ship Game Children sit in a circle to make a "flying saucer." Pantomime putting on space suits, helmets, boots, and oxygen tanks. Everyone sings to "Ring Around the Rosie" tune: We're in our spaceship, we're ready to go! Ready for the countdown, say it slow! Chant: Five-Four-Three-Two-One—BLASTOFF!! (Shake arms like it's bumpy!) Visit planets and make up movements in between verses. Repeat space ship song after each planet visit. *Examples:* Moon: Move like you're floating. Mars: Move like you're stuck. Jello planet: Move like you're walking in jello. Water planet: Move like you're swimming. Lava planet: Move like you're jumping over rivers of hot lava! Have children create planets. Ring a bell when "oxygen is running out." Everyone gets back into circle formation to sing space ship take-off song and then go to another planet. They loved this one!	Ages 4–7

Movement with Props
(Hoops, Scarves, Bean Bags)

Activity or Game	Prop	Age or Grade Level
Example: Magical Hoop Game Place hoops on the floor. Play lively music and have the children "dance" around the room. When the music stops, everyone has to get in a hoop. Take away one or two hoops. The children in those hoops are not "out." Repeat the dancing, but this time, children will have to share a hoop. Keep taking away hoops until only one remains and everyone has to get into it! Everyone wins in this game. Only the hoops get "out."	Hula hoops	Preschool–Grade 3

Recordings to Note

Name of CD or Album	Song/Activity	Age or Grade Level
Example: Hap Palmer, *Getting to Know Myself.*	"Sammy." Children move like the character in the song—fly like a bird, hop like a bunny, crawl like a bug, etc. A favorite!	Ages 3–5

Music Interest Centers

Center or Activity	Age or Grade Level
Example: Sound boxes Ms. K's class had a large box that one child could go inside. On the walls were various items that made contrasting sounds, including zippers, Velcro®, tin cans, corrugated cardboard, sandpaper and scrapers, and stretched-out rubber bands. Hanging from the top were bells, wind chimes, and shakers. Bubble wrap to pop was also attached to the walls. The child would go into the box and explore all of the sounds.	Ages 3–5

Using Instruments with Children

Activity	Age or Grade Level
Example: Ms. K's class used rhythm instruments with children's literature. She read the book *The Little Old Lady Who Was Not Afraid of Anything* (Williams, 1986) and the children played instruments to represent the parts of the pumpkin head that follow the old lady home. For example, "two shoes go clomp-clomp"—a group of children played the drum to represent the "clomp" sound. Other sounds included "wiggle," "shake," "clap," "nod," and "boo." The story was much more lively using the instruments to represent the sound effects.	K

Children's Literature: Music

Title	Author	Publisher/Date/ISBN	Age or Grade Level	Music Concepts
Example: *The Wheels on the Bus*	Maryann Kovalski	Scott Foresman 1990 ISBN: 0316502596	Ages 3–7	The story follows the popular song. Have the children choose instruments that make the many sounds made in the book, such as "swish," "toot," "clink," "waa," and "shh."

Teacher Resource Books: Music and Movement

Title	Author	Publisher/Date/ISBN	Age or Grade Level	Notes
Example: *Musical Games, Fingerplays, and Rhythmic Activities for Early Childhood*	M. Wirth, P. Stemmler, and V. Stassevitch	Parker 1983 ISBN: 013607085X	Ages 3–8	A classic collection of children's play party songs and games, popular fingerplays, and chants. The book is easy to read with suggestions for use of each song or game. Filled with hundreds of ideas!

CHAPTER 3

JOURNAL OF IDEAS
Language Arts

WHO TO OBSERVE:

- Cooperating teachers
- Assistants
- Reading teachers
- Speech therapists
- Special education teachers

IDEA PAGES:

- **Creative Drama:** What stories have you observed being acted out or pantomimed?
- **Children's Literature:** Books to remember! Write down all those stories the children enjoyed. Include the ISBN number for ease in ordering.
- **Emergent Literacy in Early Childhood Settings:** How have you seen teachers using print in the classroom? Poetry? Include favorite poems and activities.
- **Alphabet: Effective Teaching Strategies.** Include songs, games, and activities to help children identify letters and sounds.

- **Spelling and Word Games:** Write down those helpful activity ideas for spelling in the primary grades.
- **Writing Activities:** Include story starters, activities, related activities, class books, and creative ideas to encourage children to write.
- **Author Studies:** How have teachers introduced authors to the children?
- **Ideas and Advice on Teaching Reading in K–2:** What advice did professionals give you? List teacher resource books you found helpful.

Creative Drama

Story or Play to Reenact	Age or Grade Level
Example: Mrs. K's class acted out the "Three Billy Goats Gruff." The teacher narrated the story and the children pantomimed the parts. They repeated the line "trip-trap, trip-trap." Simple costumes and props included "horns," a troll hat, steps for the bridge, and a green rug for the grassy knoll.	Ages 3–5
Example for older children: Mrs. W's class put on a play about the food pyramid. Each child made a costume to represent a food in one of the food groups. For example, one child was broccoli. They presented their pyramid in the auditorium by standing on choir risers. They sang some songs about foods. After the show, each parent brought in a food treat made from the real food their child represented and they all had a feast.	Grades 1–2

Children's Literature: Language Arts

Title	Author	Publisher/Date/ISBN	Age or Grade Level	Related Activity
Example: *It Looked Like Spilt Milk*	Charles Shaw	Harper Collins 1993 ISBN: 069400491X	Ages 3–5	Make puffy paint out of ½ glue and ½ shaving cream. Have each child paint clouds onto blue paper to make a class book.

Emergent Literacy in Early Childhood Settings

Description of how you have seen teachers use print in the classroom	Age or Grade Level
Example: In Mrs. H's preschool class, the children were aware that a new president had been elected. Building on their curiosity, she suggested that the class compose a letter to the president. On large chart paper, Mrs. H wrote each question asked by a child as they dictated to her. For example, Joey asked, "Does your mother sleep in the White House, too?" After all the children had dictated their questions, she folded the letter up and mailed it to the White House. The class later received a photo of the president and a letter thanking them for their questions. Even though the children couldn't yet write, they learned that their ideas could be written down in a letter.	Ages 4–5

Poetry: Creative Activities

Activity Observed	Age or Grade Level
Example: The children in Mrs. C's class made patterned poems. The words to the poems created the pictures, such as this kite: kites fly high up in the sky soaring, soaring fly fly fly fly fly fly string bostring bostring kite kite kite kite kite kite fly fly fly fly fly kites up in the sky, by and by, I love	Grades 1–2

Favorite Poems

Words and Author of Poem	Words and Author of Poem
Classic Nursery Rhyme: *Dr. Foster* Dr. Foster went to Gloucester In a shower of rain. He stepped in a puddle, Right up to his middle! And he never went there again! Movement idea for the poem: Line 1: Pat legs to the beat of walking. Line 2: Wiggle fingers from high to low to make rain. Line 3: Jump into a hula hoop. Line 4: Pull hoop up to waist. Line 5: On the word "never," drop hoop to the floor and stamp off. As a choral reading: Use different tones of voice for each line: Lines 1 and 2: Whisper Line 3: Regular speaking voice. Line 4: Sing-song voice. Line 5: Shout! Try this in reverse as well!	

Alphabet: Effective Teaching Strategies K–2

Teaching Strategy	Age or Grade Level
Example: Mr. S nailed three cookie sheets to the wall at the children's eye level. He placed magnetic letters on each of them. The children enjoyed exploring the alphabet during free play with this simple tool. Some even tried to make up words.	Grades K–2

Spelling and Word Games

Activity Observed	Age or Grade Level
Example: Fill a cookie sheet with sand or salt. Have the children trace their spelling words in the sand and then erase for the next word. As a game, the teacher says the word and the children trace it in the sand without looking at their sheet.	Grade 2
Example: Mrs. B's class used alphabet cookie cutters to cut out their spelling words in play dough.	Grade 1

Sight Words and Word-Wall Ideas

Observation	Age or Grade Level
Example: Mrs. B printed sight words onto gray construction paper circles. She taped them to the floor with clear contact paper. When the children line up, they step on the "word stones" and say each word as they go out the door. the and at in	K

Writing Activities

Activity Observed	Age or Grade Level

Author Studies

Project Observed	Age or Grade Level
Example: Mrs. A's class studied the author Eric Carle. They read all of his books and analyzed his artwork. They each learned how to create his collage pictures and made their own (some were tissue paper, some were finger paintings cut into collage shapes). They compared and contrasted the stories and made lists of his special features.	Grade 1

Teacher Resource Books: Language Arts

Title	Author	Publisher/Date/ISBN	Age or Grade Level	Notes
Example: *Learning to Read and Write: Developmentally Appropriate Practices for Young Children*	S.B. Neuman, C. Copple, and S. Bredekamp	NAEYC 2000 ISBN: 0935989870	Infant through elementary ages	This book promotes early literacy for infant/toddler settings through elementary grades. Includes ideas and guidance for teachers. Also included in the book is NAEYC's joint position statement with the International Reading Association on best practices in reading and writing and emergent literacy.

Dog

Teacher	Advice	Age or Grade Level

CHAPTER 4

JOURNAL OF IDEAS
Social Studies

WHO TO OBSERVE:

- Cooperating teachers
- Assistants
- Special education teachers
- Parents, grandparents, guests

IDEA PAGES:

- **Activities about Self and Family:** A good social studies curriculum begins with the child and his or her family. What activities have you seen that promote a concept of self and explore family relationships?

- **Cultural Activities:** Include activities where children learn about other countries, cultural events, and the arts.

- **Developmentally Appropriate Holiday Activities:** Keeping art creative, how have teachers respectfully presented holidays?

- **Field Trip Ideas:** What field trips were successful? Include examples of guest speakers to bring into the classroom as well.

- **Dramatic Play Prop Boxes:** List all the props teachers have set out for children to role-play community helpers.

- **Teaching Geography and Mapping:** Describe activities you have observed in these areas.

- **Teaching Historical Events in Primary Grades:** Describe projects and activities you have observed.

- **Children's Literature:** What books have you found that promote social studies concepts? Also list good teacher resource books.

Self and Family: Activities/Centers

Activity or Center Observed	Concept	Age or Grade Level
Example: Mrs. A's class made family mobiles. A photo of the child was in the center and hanging all around him or her were parents, siblings, grandparents, and pets. Two wire hangers hooked together formed the actual mobile, with the mounted pictures glued to colorful paper and hung by strings. The family's last name was the lowest string. The children were very proud of their creations and talked about their families to the class.	Family	K

Cultural Activities

Activity or Center Observed	Culture or Country	Age or Grade Level
Example: Mrs. B's class was learning about Native American customs. For the art center, the children dyed strips of muslin by dipping them in bowls of cranberries and blueberries. They were surprised to see the material change color to pink and blue.	Native American	Ages 4–5

Developmentally Appropriate
Holiday Activities

Activity or Center	Holiday	Age or Grade Level
Example: Spice art For Thanksgiving, the children made collages with spices. They made designs with glue, then sprinkled cinnamon, poultry seasoning, and other spices onto the design. It smelled like turkey and apple pie.	Thanksgiving	Ages 4–6

Activity or Center	Concept	Age or Grade Level
Example: Using old boxes, cans, and packages, the children created a community consisting of a city, a suburb, and rural areas. They made buildings, streets, stop lights, houses, farms, pastures, animals, and people. (They decorated the boxes with colored construction paper.) It took up more than half the classroom. The children wrote in their journals about the part of the community they lived in.	Community	Grades 1–2

Field Trips

Field Trip	Age or Grade Level
Example: As a part of their project on shoes, the class visited two shoe stores and a shoe repair shop. When they returned, they set up their own in-class shoe store.	K

Guest Speakers/Class Visitors

Guest Speaker or Visitor	Age or Grade Level
Example: Mrs. K invited a local tow-truck driver to visit the children. He brought two tow trucks—one with a hook and one large car carrier. He drove two to three children at a time around the parking lot. They loved it! This visit began a unit on transportation.	Ages 4–5

Dramatic Play Prop Boxes

Theme	Materials	Age or Grade Level
Example: Pet store	Front desk with play cash register, play money, "uniforms," stuffed animals to sell, leashes, dog bones, water dishes, small cages made out of boxes, a dog house (made out of a box). Pictures of pets hung up, with prices of animals on signs. The children really enjoyed acting out the roles of customers, salespeople, and animals!	Ages 3–5

Geography and Mapping

Activity	Age or Grade Level
Example: Mrs. F's class made a huge world map outline that hung in the hallway. They sent letters to every student in the school asking them to have friends and families send postcards to the class as they traveled throughout the year. When a postcard arrived, the children would research the country (or state), find it on the giant map, collect and compare the stamps, and finally pin the postcard to the large world map. They received postcards from all over the world!	Grades 1–3

Teaching Historical Events

Event or Historical Figure	Activity	Age or Grade Level
Example: Martin Luther King	Mrs. D's class learned about Martin Luther King and discrimination by experiencing it firsthand. Before beginning the unit, Mrs. D sent a letter home to parents explaining what the children would be experiencing. Each child was discriminated against for something they wore. For example, Becky wore shoes with Velcro®. For that day, people who wore this type of shoe could not use the art center. All of the children experienced similar discrimination based on something they wore. At the end of the day, they talked about how it made them feel. Mrs. D then read a story about Martin Luther King and they wrote a paragraph (invented spelling) about their thoughts. It was a very moving lesson.	Grade 1

Children's Literature: Social Studies Concepts

Title	Author	Publisher/Date/ISBN	Age or Grade Level	Concepts
Example: *The Best Town in the World*	Byrd Baylor	Simon 1983 ISBN: 0684180359	Ages 3–7	Life in a town. Everything is perfect in this town as remembered by the author's father. Children can compare the story to their own towns.
Example: *Night City*	Monica Wellington	Dutton 1998 ISBN: 0525459480	Ages 3–7	Night life in a city. This book can be used to contrast with *The Best Town in the World*. The story illustrates what night workers do until dawn.

Teacher Resource Books: Social Studies

Title	Author	Publisher/Date/ISBN	Age or Grade Level	Notes
Example: *Celebrate! An Anti-bias Guide to Enjoying the Holidays*	Julie Bisson	Gryphon House 1997 ISBN: 1884834329	Preschool through elementary ages	Chapters include "Developing a Holiday Policy," "Selecting Holidays," "Addressing Stereotypes and Commercialism," and "Evaluating Holiday Activities." The book is filled with strategies to implement holiday activities that are not biased and involve families.

CHAPTER 5

JOURNAL OF IDEAS
Science

WHO TO OBSERVE:

- Cooperating teachers
- Special education teachers
- Nature guides/rangers
- Science museum staff

IDEA PAGES:

- **Discovery Centers:** Describe a discovery table.
- **Water Table Ideas:** What types of materials and props have you seen used with the water table?
- **Investigations:** Describe any investigations conducted by the children.
- **Experiments:** Describe any experiments you have seen the children work with. Include a description of the materials needed and the process involved.
- **Nature Activities:** Describe any outdoor explorations.
- **Recipes for Science Materials.**

- **Class Pets:** Make notes about the types of pets you have seen in classrooms and how to care for them.
- **Invention Centers:** What materials did you see set out to create inventions?
- **Science Books:** Include good children's literature that incorporates science concepts.
- **Science Projects and Science Fair Ideas for Elementary Age Children.**
- **Science Materials to Find or Purchase.**
- **Technology in the Classroom:** Note how teachers have used computers in instruction. Also note good software you have observed children using.

Discovery Centers

Types of Materials Observed	Age or Grade Level
Example: Texture Tray The teacher set out many different items of various textures for the children to explore, including: a piece of satin, sandpaper, corrugated cardboard, bubble wrap, pieces of metal, bark, a piece of fake fur, Plexiglas®, a Koosh® Ball, rubber dog toys, and so on.	Ages 3–5

Water Table Ideas

Types of Materials Used in Water Tables	Age or Grade Level
Example: Mrs. C put birdseed in her water table. The children loved the texture.	Ages 3–5

Investigations

Type of Investigation Conducted by Children	Age or Grade Level
Example: The children in Mrs. P's class were studying ants. They went outside with magnifying glasses and investigated the ant hills on the playground. They drew pictures of the ants and wrote a journal about what they observed the ants actually doing. Once back in the classroom, they compared their drawings to photos of real ants to determine what type of ant they had seen. They listed characteristics of ants and wrote a summary of their findings	Grades 2–3

Experiments

Description of Experiments Observed	Age or Grade Level
Example: Miss A's class studied static electricity. First, they made predictions about what would happen if you rub a balloon on different things. Then they explored four different stations. The first group rubbed a balloon on their friend's head and then wrote what happened (hair stood on end). The next group rubbed a balloon on the carpet and then held it over a bowl of rice cereal (cereal jumped out of bowl to balloon). The next group rubbed the balloon on the carpet and then held it over some sprinkled salt and pepper (which also jumped up). The last group rubbed the balloon on the floor (or on their hair) and put the balloon on the wall (it stuck). They were very engaged in finding out what would happen. They learned the words "static electricity" and "charged."	Grades 1–2

Nature Activities

Examples of Outdoor Activities Observed	Age or Grade Level
Example: While on a nature walk, Ms. K gave each child a paint chip palette (from a paint store). The children had to find something in nature that matched one of their paint chips. This activity helped their observation skills and they also really enjoyed it.	Ages 4–5 Grades 1–3

Recipes for Science Materials

Example: "Goop"

Mix cornstarch and water together in a bowl. Consistency should be hard and wet at the same time. Children are fascinated when exploring the mixture's properties. Even though it looks wet, it is hard. Have the children punch it. If you push your finger in slowly, it becomes soft like a liquid. Have them try to pick it up. At first it is solid, but then it turns to liquid and drips out of your hand!
Good for ages 2–7.

Class Pets

Type of Animal	Life Span	Type of Home	Food	Notes
Example: Gerbils	2 years	Cage or aquarium with screened top. Gerbils need to chew. Give them toilet paper rolls and thin boxes. They will shred them up to create a nest. Ms. K's gerbils loved egg cartons.	Hamster & gerbil food. They also like fresh vegetables. Their favorite food is sunflower seeds. (But too many make them sick.)	They require very little care. Do not get hamster-type toys, as their tails could get caught. Commercially made gerbil balls are clear and the gerbils can safely run all over in them.

Invention Centers

Center Observed	Age or Grade Level
Example: Mrs. B's class had a center for making robots. No models were used. She labeled the area "ROBOT CENTER" and simply provided open-ended materials. These included rolls of foil, rolls of masking and cellophane tape, staplers, paper in all colors, boxes (such as cereal boxes), toilet paper rolls, paper towel rolls, newspapers, film canisters, oatmeal boxes, and cellophane. The children made many exciting and creative robots.	Grades K–2

Children's Literature: Science Concepts

Author	Title	Publisher/Date/ISBN	Age or Grade Level	Science Concepts
Example: Tomie dePaola	*Cloud Book*	Scholastic 1979 ISBN: 059008531X	Grades 1–2	Teaches about the different types of clouds.

Science Projects and Science Fair Ideas

Project Observed	Age or Grade Level
Example: Mrs. P's class was learning about the solar system. The children made papier-mâché planets with balloons as the base. The children tore strips of newspaper and dipped them into a mixture of flour and water (felt like lumpy oatmeal). They then wrapped the strips around the balloons, smoothing away the flour mixture as they worked. They tied strings to the ends of the balloons and hung them from the ceiling to dry. After a few days, they popped the balloons inside and painted the exteriors as the planet of their choice. In the process, the children learned to compare the sizes and features of the various planets and planetary bodies. The children researched their chosen planet in the library and on the Internet.	Grades 2–3

The Scientific Method

Observation	Age or Grade Level
Example: Mrs. H encourages her first graders to be "scientists." She put a poster on the wall that read: Be a Scientist! • Wonder • Observe • Predict • Record and tell • Experiment Whenever she does a science project in class, Mrs. H reviews these steps with the children. For example, they planted seeds one day. They discussed the seeds, made predictions about what would happen, planted and watered the seeds, and then kept a plant journal as they observed their plants grow each day. After two weeks, they wrote a small report telling about what happened to their plant.	Ages 4–9

Science Materials to Find or Purchase

Type of Material	Where to Find or Purchase	Use
Example: Magnetic Marbles	Discount School Supply P. O. Box 7636 Spreckels, CA 93962 www.discountschoolsupply.com 1-800-627-2829	Units on magnets. Magnetic marble rolling—put the marbles in a box with splotches of paint. Drag the magnet wand under the box. Children are amazed to see the marbles move through the paint!

Technology in the Classroom

Observation of Computer Use	Age or Grade Level
Example: Mrs. A's class used their computer to send e-mail messages to their pen pals in Australia! They learned how to write a letter and asked questions about life as a second grader there. One question was, "Do you have a pet kangaroo?" They also learned how to use the Internet and e-mail by participating in this project, which lasted the whole year.	Grade 2

Computer Software to Note

Name of Program	Description	Age or Grade Level
Example: Blue's Birthday Adventure Windows 95/98/Mac	Similar to the television show *Blue's Clues,* the child collects clues and inserts them into the "Handy Dandy Notebook." There are multiple clickable objects and hidden objects to collect. The games are easy and fun to play and help children practice their critical thinking and logical problem-solving skills. Mrs. K's class really loved it.	Ages 3–6

Teacher Resource Books: Science

Title	Author	Publisher/Date/ISBN	Age or Grade Level	Notes
Example: *Sand and Water Play: Simple, Creative Activities for Children*	Sherrie West and Amy Cox	Gryphon House 2001 ISBN: 0876592477	Ages 3–6	This book has more than 70 ideas for sand and water play. Sample ideas for new media to use include aquarium rocks, birdseed, mud, and rock salt.

CHAPTER 6

JOURNAL OF IDEAS

Cooking and Nutrition

WHO TO OBSERVE:

- Cooperating teachers
- Assistants
- School cook
- Nutritionist

IDEA PAGES:

- **One-Cup Cooking Ideas:** How have you seen cooking presented to small groups of children? Include any recipes, drawings of recipe cards for the children, and materials needed. A good source for cup cooking ideas is the following book: Foote, B. J. (2001). *Cup cooking: Individual child-portion picture recipes.* Gainesville, MD: Gryphon House. ISBN 0960439048.

- **Whole-Group Cooking Ideas:** How have you seen cooking presented to large groups of children? Record the process and recipes.

- **Nutritional Activities:** How have you observed teachers promoting good nutrition in the classroom? Activities on the food pyramid?

- **Healthy Snacks:** Here's a place to write down those creative snacks you've seen and tasted!

- **Cooking Resource Books for Teachers:** List good cookbooks for children and cooking activity books you have found.

"One-Cup" Cooking Ideas

Note: One-cup cooking is a method in which the child completes all steps in a recipe by following a series of recipe "cards" from left to right. This works well as a center for groups of one to four children. It promotes prereading skills as the child literally moves through the process from left to right. Picture cards encourage word and numeral recognition.

Example Recipe: English Muffin Pizzas

1. Wash hands!

2. Take one muffin and place it on paper plate.

3. Spread one spoonful of sauce on muffin.

4. Take two spoonfuls of cheese and sprinkle on sauce.

5. Place one pepperoni on top of cheese.

6. Place muffin on cookie sheet.

7. Write name with permanent marker on foil under muffin.

8. When tray is full, bake at 325° until cheese melts.

Materials Needed:
Six-pack of English muffins (broken in half)
Jar of tomato (or pizza) sauce
12 oz. bag of shredded mozzarella
Bag of sliced pepperoni
Two cookie sheets with foil
Bowl for the mozzarella
Bowl for the pepperoni
12 plastic spoons for spreading sauce
Sandwich bags for recipe cards
Paper plates
Napkins
Large spoon (or tongs) for mozzarella
Foil
Permanent marker

Child's Recipe Cards to "Read":

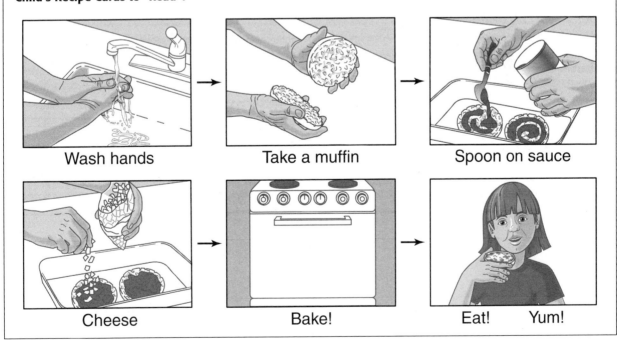

Wash hands   Take a muffin   Spoon on sauce

Cheese   Bake!   Eat!   Yum!

"One-Cup" Cooking Activities

Recipe: _____

Serves: _____

Materials Needed:

Child's Recipe Cards to "Read":

Whole-Group Cooking Ideas

Example Recipe: No-Bake Banana Muffins in a Cup

Serves: *24*

Follow directions for muffins on box of banana bread mix. Each child takes a turn to put in and mix ingredients. Fill paper cups half full with mixture. Place all of the cups side by side inside the electric frying pan. Set at 350°. Put cover on top. Let the muffins "bake" for 20–35 minutes until brown on top. (Check frequently.) Carefully remove from frying pan. Teacher peels off the cup from the muffin.

Materials Needed:
Box of banana bread mix
2 eggs
Oil (use amount stated on mix)
Milk (use amount stated on mix)
Paper cups (wax coated)
Electric frying pan
Mixing bowl, spoons, measuring spoons, and cup
Oven mitt

Notes: This works well when there is no oven available. The children were amazed that the paper cups did not burn. Cut into the paper cup for easier peeling.

Recipe: _____
Serves: _____

Materials Needed:

Notes:

Whole-Group Cooking Ideas

Recipe: _____
Serves: _____

Materials Needed:

Notes:

Recipe: _____
Serves: _____

Materials Needed:

Notes:

Nutrition Activities

Activity Observed	Age or Grade Level
Example: The children were learning about the food pyramid. The teacher drew a large pyramid on heavy chart paper. The children cut out pictures of healthy foods from magazines and glued them into the appropriate category on the pyramid. As a follow-up, the children then glued healthy foods onto a plate, with an example from each food group to represent a meal.	K

Healthy Snacks

Healthy Snack or Recipe	Age or Grade Level
Example: Ants on a Log Cut up pieces of celery, add peanut butter or cream cheese, and top with raisins.	Ages 3–5

Children's Literature: Cooking and Nutrition

Title	Author	Publisher/Date/ISBN	Age or Grade Level	Summary
Example: *Bread and Jam for Frances*	Russell Hoban and Lillian Hoban	Harper Trophy 1993 (new edition) ISBN: 0064430960	Ages 3–7	Classic children's story about Frances, who insists on eating nothing but bread and jam until she realizes her parents are no longer noticing! Great for picky eaters!

Cookbooks for Children

Title	Author	Publisher/Date/ISBN	Age or Grade Level	Notes
Example: *The Healthy Start Kids Cookbook*	Sandra Nissenberg	John Wiley 1994 ISBN: 0471347337	Ages 6–10	This book includes 90 recipes approved by parents and a nutritionist. Examples include "Painted Pancakes," "Fruit Kabobs," and "Gingerbread Muffins." Includes safety tips, step-by-step instructions, utensil listings, and nutrition information.
Example: *Pretend Soup and Other Real Recipes: A Cookbook for Preschoolers and Up.*	M. Katzen and A. Henderson	Tricycle Press 1994 ISBN: 1883672066	Ages 4–8	Includes 17 recipes that are repeated once in words and once in pictures. All are nutritious and fun to make.

Teacher Resource Books:
Cooking and Nutrition

Title	Author	Publisher/Date/ISBN	Age or Grade Level	Notes
Example: *Nutrition Activities for Preschoolers*	A. Ray, T. Harms, and D. Cryer	Pearson Learning 1996 ISBN: 0201494523	Preschool	Activities are tied to learning centers such as blocks, books, pretend play, science, math, art, music, and so on. Includes information on good nutrition.

CHAPTER 7

JOURNAL OF IDEAS
Math

WHO TO OBSERVE:

- Cooperating teachers
- Special education teachers
- Math resource teachers

IDEA PAGES:

- **Math Concept Development:** Write down how you have seen teachers indirectly and directly encourage the concepts of counting, number, shape and form, classification, seriation, ordinal numbers, and size and measurement.

- **Patterning:** Describe patterning activities. Include block play ideas.

- **Graphing Activities:** How have you seen teachers indirectly and directly teach graphing to children?

- **Calendar Activities and Routines for K–2:** What developmentally appropriate calendar activities have you observed?

- **Money Concepts:** How have you seen elementary teachers develop this concept?

- **The 100th Day of School:** A popular event for kindergarten classes! What special activities did you observe?

- **Telling Time:** How have you seen elementary teachers help children develop this concept? Include ideas for sequencing events for preschoolers, such as planning boards.

- **Adding, Subtracting, and Place Value:** How have you seen children developing these skills?

- **Math Games and Materials:** Make note of commercial and homemade math materials for future reference.

- **Children's Books with Math Concepts:** There are many wonderful counting books for children. List those the children have enjoyed.

Counting, Cardinal Numbers, and Numerals

Activity Observed	Age or Grade Level
Example: Mrs. R numbered the tables in her kindergarten classroom. In the beginning of the year, the tables were numbered 1, 2, 3, and 4. "Table 4 line up" and so on. Every month, she would change the numerals on the tables. In March, the tables were numbered 13, 14, 15, and 16. This really helped the children recognize these numerals.	K

Ordinal Numbers (First, Second, Third...)

Activity Observed	Age or Grade Level
Example: Mrs. W taught ordinal numbers in an indirect manner during line-up for lunch. She said, "The first person in line has blue eyes, a red shirt, and a name that starts with J." "The second person in line is wearing a purple top with a cat on it!" She continued this way for each child in the class. When all were lined up, she asked them to tell her what order they were in. Child one said "first," the next, "second," and so on.	Grades K–2

Shape and Form

Activity, Material, or Game Observed	Age or Grade Level
Example: The children in Ms. K's class learned about shape and form by creating shape sculptures out of rolled-up newspaper. The children rolled the paper tightly from the top right corner to the lower left corner. Next they taped it together. It looked like a paper stick. Using tape, they shaped these "paper sticks" into three dimensional objects.	K

Classification and Seriation (Order) Activities

Activity Observed	Age or Grade Level
Example: The children were given a bowl of colorful beads of varying sizes. The teacher gave them tongs and muffin tins. They had a great time sorting out the different types of beads into the different sections of the muffin tin. Some of the children also seriated them from smallest to largest.	Grade 1

Size and Measurement

Activity Observed	Age or Grade Level
Example: The children measured each other using different objects as units of measurement. Examples: unit blocks, Legos®, hands (like horses), milk cartons, and so on. Amy exclaimed, "I'm 10 blocks tall!"	Ages 4–7
Example: As a part of a dinosaur unit, the children measured out the length of a brontosaurus by putting tape on the floor of the school hallway to represent its size from tail to nose. It was as long as the whole school building! They also discovered that a T-rex is as long as three school buses! Relating size of objects to real things seemed to help the children understand just how big these creatures really were.	Grade 1

Patterning

Activity Observed	Age or Grade Level
Example: *Friendship quilt:* Give the children a square of construction paper in the color of their choice. Fold it in half and cut lines from the fold out to the edge, but don't go all the way—leave one inch at the end. Cut strips of paper in different colors and weave these (over, under) through the cut strips. The children created their own patterns using different colors for each line. When they were finished, all of the pattern squares were glued onto a large piece of paper to create a class "friendship quilt." This activity integrated math, art, and social studies.	Grade 1

Block Play

Observation	Age or Grade Level
Example: Mrs. C's class had an extensive block area. All of the blocks were neatly stored on child-sized bookshelves. A colored cut-out of each block was laminated onto the shelf so the child could match the actual block to its location on the shelf at clean-up time. Many props were provided for block play, including toy animals and small cars and trucks. To encourage problem solving, Mrs. C used masking tape to make a square on the rug and challenged children to try to build something that fit in the square. The buildings the children made were very creative!	Preschool–Grade 1

Graphing Activities

Activity Observed (Direct or Indirect)	Age or Grade Level
Example: Indirect Graphing Activity On the blackboard, Mrs. A made three columns out of masking tape labeled "Hot Lunch," "Sandwich," and "Lunch from Home." When the children arrived in the morning, they found their name on a magnetized card and placed it under the appropriate column. During morning meeting, the teacher reviewed the columns, pointing out which choice had the most, the least, etc. In this case, graphing was a regular part of the morning routine.	Grade 1
Example: Direct Graphing Activity The children visited an apple orchard and brought back many different types of apples. They cut them up into small pieces and had a taste-testing party. The children (with the teacher's help) made a large graph with drawings of the different apples across the top (Delicious, Macintosh, Granny Smith, etc.). The children glued a square with their name on it for the apple they liked the best. Together, they counted the columns and determined the favorite apple of the class. In this case, the children were learning how to design and use graphs.	K

Money Concepts

Observation	Age or Grade Level
Example: Mrs. B's kindergartners had a class store. Every morning when they arrived, they found a bowl of real coins on their tables. They needed to find the exact change to purchase an item from the store. For example, a sticker cost 17 cents, so the child needed to find a dime, a nickel, and two pennies. What a hit!	Grades K–2

Calendar Activities and Routines for K–2

Activity or Routine Observed	Age or Grade Level
Example: After the class counted out the days in the month, they also noted how many days they had been going to school. The "calendar child" of the day wrote the numeral on an index card and hung it on the wall next to the previous day's number, creating a number line. The whole class counted from 1 to the present day of the year. On day 100, they had a big celebration!	Grades K–2

100th Day of School Activities

Activity Observed	Age or Grade Level
Example: During 100-day festivities, the children participated in a variety of activities to experience the number 100. One group counted to 100 by doing 100 jumping jacks, hops in place, and jump roping. They were exhausted! They said "100 is a lot!"	K

Telling Time

Activity Observed	Age or Grade Level
Example: Miss M made a giant clock on the floor. Children were given cards with a digital time, such as 12:15. Two children would create the time on the clock. One child sat on the 12, and one sat on the 3. They both made the hands point to the appropriate number. They really enjoyed being a part of the clock and frequently asked to repeat the game.	Grade 2

Adding and Subtracting:

Activity Observed	Age or Grade Level
Example: Miss M had the children work with a partner to create double-digit subtraction problems. One child would roll the dice twice to create the first number. The second child rolled the dice for the second number. The two children had to decide which number was larger to put on the top. Then they solved the problem together. They really seemed to enjoy this activity!	Grade 2

Place Value

Activity Observed	Age or Grade Level
Example: In Mrs. A's class, the children were learning how to create a model of a two-digit number using a place-value board. The place-value board had two columns: one for 10s and one for 1s. The children chose a number out of a hat, in this case, 37. The children were given a number of sticks to count. Whenever they got to 10, they were to wrap the sticks up with a rubber band. Each group of 10 sticks was placed under the 10s column on a poster-board chart. The remaining sticks were placed under the 1s column. The children then wrote out the number. For example, three bundles of 10s = 30 and 7 sticks left would equal the number 37.	Grades 1–2

Math Games and Materials

Description of Math Material or Game	Age or Grade Level
Example: Mrs. B made a game for her addition math center. She made a prop that had four tunnels cut out. A numeral was written over the top of each tunnel. The child rolled a marble toward the tunnel. He or she would write down the number of the tunnel that the marble rolled through. He or she would repeat this and then add the two numbers together using counters. The children loved this game!	K
Example: Mrs. W made her own giant dice out of small milk cartons. She wrote a numeral on each of the six sides of card stock she had taped to the milk carton. When finished, she covered the entire "die" with clear Con-Tact® paper. Children would roll the two dice and add up the numbers!	Grades K–1

Children's Literature: Math Concepts

Title	Author	Publisher/Date/ISBN	Age or Grade Level	Concepts
Example: *The Grouchy Ladybug*	Eric Carle	Scott/Foresman 1996 ISBN: 0064434508	Ages 3–7	Time, size, seriation

Teacher Resource Books: Math

Title	Author	Publisher/Date/ISBN	Age or Grade Level	Notes
Example: *The Young Child and Mathematics*	Juanita V. Copley	NAEYC 2000 ISBN: 0935989978	Preschool through Grade 2	This book is based on National Association for the Education of Young Children (NAEYC) guidelines and the National Council of Teachers of Mathematics standards. It offers activities and strategies to make math exciting for children in preschool and primary classes.

CHAPTER 8

JOURNAL OF IDEAS

Motor Development

WHO TO OBSERVE:

- Cooperative teachers
- Assistants
- Special education teachers
- Physical education teachers
- Physical therapists
- Occupational therapists
- Recreational therapists

IDEA PAGES:

- **Activities for Fine Motor Development:**
  Describe centers, toys, and activities you have
  seen that help children develop fine motor skills.
  Also include activities to improve writing skills for
  elementary children.

- **Activities for Gross Motor Development:**
  Describe indoor and outdoor games and
  activities that help children develop gross motor
  skills.

- **Playground Play:** What types of play (either
  indirect or direct) did you observe on the
  playground?

- **Outdoor Water Play:** Describe toys, props,
  and activities for outdoor water play.

- **Outdoor Play Equipment:** Draw or describe
  types of equipment you'd like for your own
  school.

Fine Motor Activities

Observation	Age or Grade Level
Example: Children were delighted with this simple center that helped fine motor development. The teacher put a bag of pom-poms into a bowl. The sizes ranged from very tiny to large. The children used all sorts of tongs to pick up the pom-poms and move them from the bowl to muffin tins. Some children sorted them by size or color, but most seemed to concentrate on using the tongs. A very popular center!	Ages 4–5

Fine Motor Development: Writing

Observation	Age or Grade Level
Example: Miss S, the occupational therapist, recommended having the kindergartners do the following activities as prewriting warm-ups: • *"Inchworm":* Have the child hold the pencil near the eraser with a pincer grasp (thumb and forefinger). Next have the child inch their fingers down the pencil and back up. • *"Helicopter":* Spin a pencil held horizontally between thumb and first two fingers. • *"Windmill":* Do the same, except hold the pencil vertically. Finish the warm-up by snapping fingers. The children are now ready to write!	K

94

Gross Motor Activities and Games

Activity or Game Observed	Age or Grade Level
Example: This game was played outside on a field by a first-grade class. The teacher set up a perimeter that the children needed to stay inside. Each child found a partner. One of the children was the "chaser" and the other child was "it." The chasers had to spin in place three times while the children who were "it" started to run around the field. The chasers then got to run after their partner. With all of the children in one area, it was hard to find the one person who was "it"! When the child tagged their partner, they switched roles, beginning again with the tagged child spinning in place three times. They loved this game.	Grades 1–5

Playground Play

Observation, Game, or Activity	Age or Grade Level
Example: Mrs. K sprinkled sequins in the mulch on the playground. She told the children that there was hidden treasure to be found! The children ran all over the playground searching for the sparkling sequins. This activity also promoted their fine motor development, as they needed to use a pincer grasp to pick up the small pieces. It also refined their observation skills. The teacher had a small "treasure box" for the children to deposit their finds in! What a hit!	Ages 3–5

Outdoor Water Play

Observation	Age or Grade Level
Example: The teacher provided the children with buckets of water and medium-sized painters' brushes. The children "painted" the walls, doors, and sidewalks of the school building. The water made it look like they were changing the color of the object being painted ! They really enjoyed this.	Ages 2–6

Outdoor Sandbox Play

Observation	Age or Grade Level
Example: Miss O noticed that her preschool class was becoming bored with the sandbox. She purchased about 20 silk-flower sets from the dollar store and set up a small "flower shop" near the sandbox. The children were excited about "buying" the flowers and they spent hours planting them in the sand.	Preschool

Outdoor Play Equipment

Description of Equipment	Uses	Age or Grade Level
Example: A father made this "tightrope walk" for the playground: He cut an old hose into two eight-foot pieces. Inside each, he inserted a heavy chain that he bolted to two sides of the playground climber. At the children's arm level, he nailed two boards to serve as hand rails.	The child walks on the hose. There is an implied sense of peril, even though the child is only a few inches above the ground. This helps promote balance and self-esteem.	Ages 3–6

Teacher Resource Books: Motor Development

Title	Author	Publisher/Date/ISBN	Age or Grade Level	Notes
Example: *The Second Cooperative Sports Book: Challenge Without Competition.*	Terry Orlick	Random House 1982 ISBN: 0394748131	Infants through adult	This wonderful resource is filled with noncompetitive games. Everyone wins in the games found here. These activities encourage children to work together rather than against each other. The book also includes a discussion on games from other cultures. Filled with more than 250 games for all ages.

CHAPTER 9

JOURNAL OF IDEAS

Integrated Curriculum

WHO TO OBSERVE:

- Cooperating teachers
- Assistant teachers
- Special subject teachers
- Special education teachers

IDEA PAGES:

- **Webbing Pages:** Pages are available to sketch out your own theme or unit ideas. Begin with concept webs—brainstorm all the concepts you hope to develop over the course of a theme or unit. Turn these ideas into activities and centers (see next section).

- **Themes or Units:** Space is provided to record 10 themes or units. List activities that developed from your webbing, or record noteworthy themes or units you have observed. Remember that additional space is available to record your

activities for the unit in more detail in each chapter of this book.

- **Project Approach:** Space is provided to record projects you observed or implemented, including all of the phases. If you are interested in learning about this approach, visit www.project-approach.com for examples of projects.

- **Teacher Resource Books:** List all of the worthwhile theme or curriculum books you have reviewed.

Concept Web Example

(Use this to brainstorm)

Live Near Water
People
Polar bears
Beavers
Seals

Weather
Rain Clouds
Snow
Sleet
Ice
Fog

Water Bodies
Ocean River
Pond Puddle
Lake Sea
Stream
River

WATER

Jobs
Firefighter
Lifeguard
Sailor
Fisherperson
Cook

Water Use
Shower Bath
Clean dishes
Swim Drink
Water plants

Properties
Wet
Clear
Liquid
Solid–Ice
Vapor–Steam

Live in Water
Fish Turtles
Dolphins
Whales Sharks
Jellyfish
Snails

Concept Web Form

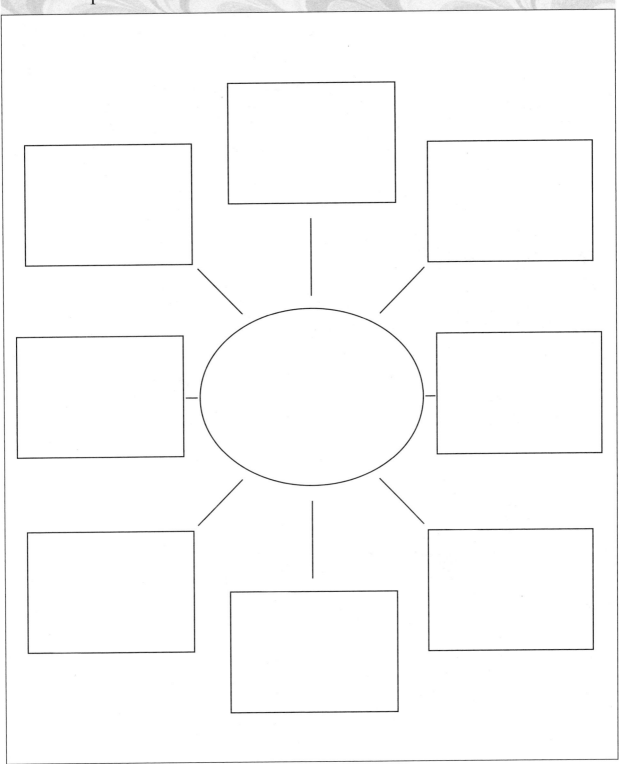

Need extra forms? Download this page at http://www.earlychilded.delmar.com

Theme or Unit Example

Theme or Unit: Water

Note: Outline your theme here. Write out the details of the activities in the chapters of this book. Reference the page here.

Art:
- **Painting with water:** Bring brushes and pails of water outside and "paint" the building.
- **Centers:** Watercolor painting
- **Centers:** Using eye droppers, drop colored water onto coffee filters. Use only primary colors (red, blue, and yellow) so the children can discover the secondary colors (purple, green, and orange.)

Music, Songs, and Finger Plays:
- **Create a thunderstorm** using rhythm instruments. Have children create sounds for rain, heavy rain, thunder, and wind.
- **Chant: Dr. Foster Went to Gloucester.** Act out "shower of rain" and "stepping in a puddle." (See p. 28 for chant)
- **Sing "Row, Row, Row Your Boat."** Sit on floor with partners and rock back and forth.

Science Center:
- **Observe and record** what happens when an ice cube melts. (In the winter, if possible, also try this with snow.)
- **Plant experiment:** Plant cups with flower seeds. Water half the seeds regularly and don't water the other seeds. Observe and record what happens.
- **Display posters of marine life:** whales, dolphin, fish, sharks, jellyfish, etc.

Math/Manipulatives/Blocks:
- Put out ocean and beach, rain and firefighter **puzzle sets**.
- **Explore which objects will sink or float.** Use manipulatives, foam blocks, wood blocks, cork, rocks, sponges, large beads, balls.
- **Put toy boats in the block area.**

Dramatic Play:
- **Set up a firehouse prop box.** Include firefighter outfits, hats, hoses (paper-towel tubes), play truck made out of a box, bells to ring, and toy siren. Make pretend fire out of red and yellow cellophane paper. Put out toy fire hydrant.
- Have water available in **toy tubs to wash babies**.

Children's Literature/Language:
- Lionni, L. (1970). *Fish is Fish.* New York: Pantheon.
- Green, C. (1982). *Rain, Rain.* Chicago: Children's.
- Keller, H. (1984). *Will it Rain?* New York: Greenwillow.
- Martin, B., & Archambault, J. (1988). *Listen to the Rain.* New York: Holt.
- McMillan, B. (1988). *Dry or Wet?* New York: Lothrop.

Sand/Water Table:
- **Pouring and measuring:** Add to the water table plastic measuring cups, funnels, squirt bottles, rubber tubes, sponges, straws, egg beaters, eye droppers, and basters. Put a few drops of blue liquid watercolor in the water to make it look like the ocean.
- **Sand table:** Add a bucket of water to experiment with what will happen when the sand gets wet.

Outdoor Activities:
- **Take a walk on a rainy day.** Bring umbrellas and boots. Listen to the sound of the rain falling, examine puddles.
- In nice weather, **set out sprinklers** and water table.

Cooking/Healthy Snacks:
- Purchase a **cake mix** for which you only add water, such as gingerbread mix. Cook with the children and make note of the changes before and after water was added and after cooking.
- **Make lemonade:** one lemon per child, twist over juicer. Add 1 cup of cold water and ice. Add a spoonful of sugar to sweeten.

Other:
- **Field trip:** Visit the local environmental center and go on a walk around a pond. Explore the animal and plant life that live near the water. View exhibits in the center.
- **Class visitor:** Have a firefighter visit the class to demonstrate putting on his or her uniform and talk about fire safety.

Theme or Unit Form

Theme or Unit:

Art:	**Music, Songs, and Finger Plays:**
Science Center:	**Math/Manipulatives/Blocks:**
Dramatic Play:	**Children's Literature/Language:**
Sand/Water Table:	**Outdoor Activities:**
Cooking/Healthy Snacks:	**Other:**

Need extra forms? Download this page at http://www.earlychilded.delmar.com

Project Approach

Title of Project:

Phase 1: Beginning the Project (questions to investigate)

Phase 2: Developing the Project (field work, investigations, representation, and documentation)

Phase 3: Concluding the Project (culminating events)

Need extra forms? Download this page at http://www.earlychilded.delmar.com

Teacher Resource Books: Themes, Units, and Projects

Title	Author	Publisher/Date/ISBN	Age or Grade Level	Notes
Example: *Engaging Children's Minds: The Project Approach* (2nd Ed.)	L. G. Katz and S. C. Chard	Ablex 2000 ISBN: 1567505007	Preschool– elementary	An excellent resource to learn more about the project approach and how to integrate it into the curriculum. Examples of projects and phases of projects are included.
Example: *Creative Resources for the Early Childhood Classroom* (4th ed.)	J. Herr and Y. Libby-Larson	Delmar Learning 2004 ISBN: 1401825540	Preschool– elementary	This book is organized by themes and includes finger plays, songs, art activities, centers (science, math, etc.), and children's books for each topic. Includes webbing and inter- active bulletin boards. An excellent book!

CHAPTER 10

JOURNAL OF IDEAS

Observation and Assessment

WHO TO OBSERVE:

- Cooperating teachers
- Assistant teachers
- Reading teachers
- Psychologists and special educators
- Social workers and therapists

IDEA PAGES:

- **Observation Methods**. True teaching and curriculum are derived from the needs and interests of children. In this section, attach samples of observation forms and methods you have seen others using in the field. Try to include as many as possible. These will serve as a foundation for designing your own. Include:
  - Running record forms
  - Anecdotal record forms
  - Checklists
  - Reading logs
  - Attendance forms
  - Developmental checklists

  - Rating scales
  - Work samples
  - Report cards or progress report forms
  - Daily assessment sheets (infant/toddler)
  - Time samples
  - Logs
  - Frequency counts
  - Technology: digital photos, e-mail, electronic portfolios
- **Case Studies:** Space is provided for your own observations of children. Develop your own recording methods and formats here.

Observation Methods

Attach observation form here	Notes
Type of Record:	

Case Study

Date	Name of Child:

Need extra forms? Download this page at http://www.earlychilded.delmar.com

CHAPTER 11

JOURNAL OF IDEAS
Health and Safety

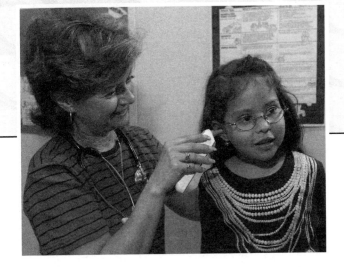

WHO TO OBSERVE:

- Cooperating teachers
- School nurse
- Directors and principals
- Safety officers (fire, police)

IDEA PAGES:

- **Health and Safety Activities:** Record activities you have observed that teach children about being safe, proper hand washing, toileting, and playground safety.
- **Fire Safety:** Make note of activities presented by firefighters. Note related activities you have observed teachers implementing. Keep a record of fire drills—make note of how teachers have kept children calm and orderly.
- **Emergency Procedures:** What happens when a child gets hurt? Review emergency procedures at your school and record the information here for future reference. Keep a record of incidents so you'll know what to do in the future. Also keep track of your own training in first aid/CPR.

- **Procedures for Keeping Children Safe and Healthy:** What have you learned or observed about universal precautions, hand washing, sanitizing, diapering, and keeping the classroom and playground safe?
- **Common Childhood Illnesses and Allergies:** Beginning teachers are often surprised by the illnesses they encounter in the field. Here's a place to record information about childhood diseases and allergies you may be unfamiliar with.
- **Children's Literature about Health and Safety:** Record children's books you have found that teach health and safety concepts. Also record useful teacher resource books.

Health and Safety Activities

Observation or Activity	Age or Grade Level
Example: Miss G noted that her first graders were not washing their hands correctly. To demonstrate the need for longer washing time, she conducted a fun activity. Each child was given a few drops of an unscented hand lotion and told to rub it into their hands. Next she sprinkled a few drops of glitter onto each hand for them to rub in. Of course, the glitter stuck to the hand lotion. The children were then directed to wash their hands until the glitter was all gone. The teacher told the children to think of the glitter as germs. How long do you have to wash your hands to get them off? The school nurse told the children to sing "Happy Birthday" while they washed! This takes about 30 seconds, long enough for a proper cleaning.	Grades 1–3

Fire Safety

Observation or Activity	Age or Grade Level
Example: Miss K invited a firefighter to visit the class. She noted that some of the children were very frightened of firefighters. In fact, children have died in fires because they have hidden from firefighters, frightened by their masks and their respirators, which make them look and sound like villains from a scary movie. Her goal was for the children to see firefighters as friends. The visitor arrived in street clothes to show the children that firefighters are simply people. He talked to the children about his job and then demonstrated the gear he wears to protect himself from fire. He started by putting on the pants, then the boots, and then the coat and hat. The children were not at all afraid. He finished with the mask and respirator, which he first allowed all the children to touch. He continually lifted the mask to reassure the children that he was still under there! This method worked very well in easing children's fears.	Preschool– kindergarten

Emergency Procedures

Type of Emergency	Procedures
Example: Seizure	I observed a child having a seizure and the first-aid procedures used by my cooperating teacher. She gave me the following list of procedures to follow in case it happens again: 1. In emergency situations, always dial 911 first! 2. Keep calm! 3. Protect the child from further injury. Try to break his or her fall, loosen any tight clothing, and turn his or her head to the side. 4. Do NOT try to restrain the child. Do NOT put anything into his or her mouth—this can cause more injury. 5. Allow the child to rest or sleep after the seizure is over with. 6. Contact the child's parents.

Procedures for Keeping Children Safe and Healthy

Topic	Procedure or Observation
Example: Universal precautions	The following health and safety guidelines were posted in the classroom: 1. Wash hands frequently. 2. Use hand lotion to prevent cracks in skin that allow germs to enter. 3. Always wear disposable latex gloves when you might come in contact with body fluids (saliva, mucus, blood, urine, feces). Remove gloves by pulling the first one off inside out and then taking the second one off to put inside that one, keeping any fluids away from your clean hands. (Wash hands again!) 4. Dispose of waste properly (diapers, bloodstained paper towels, tissues, etc.). 5. Clean surfaces with a disinfectant made of one tablespoon of bleach to one quart of water.

Common Childhood Illnesses and Allergies

Illness	Description of symptoms and treatments
Example: Ringworm	Ringworm is a mild infection of the skin or nails caused by several different fungi. It appears as a flat, growing, ring-shaped rash. It may be scaly and itchy. Note: Worms are not involved! It is treated with an antifungal medication (usually an ointment) for several weeks. Ringworm is often found on the scalp and some hair loss may be involved. Once treated, the hair grows back.

Basic First Aid and Infant/Child CPR: Notes

Training Received/Date	Notes to Remember

Children's Literature: Health and Safety Concepts

Title	Author	Publisher/Date/ISBN	Age or Grade Level	Concepts
Example: *Germs Make Me Sick*	Melvin Berger and Marylin Hafner	Harper Collins 1995 ISBN: 0064451542	Ages 5–9	Explains germs and bacteria and how they are transmitted.

Teacher Resource Books: Health and Safety

Title	Author	Publisher/Date/ISBN	Age or Grade Level	Notes
Example: *Health, Safety and Nutrition for the Young Child*	L. Marotz, J. Rush, and M. Cross.	Delmar Learning 2000 ISBN: 0766809463	Birth–elementary	This is a comprehensive text that includes everything a teacher needs to know about health, safety, and nutrition. It includes information on infection control, quality environments, accidents, injuries, and nutritional guidelines.

CHAPTER 12

JOURNAL OF IDEAS
Infants and Toddlers

WHO TO OBSERVE:

- Cooperating teachers
- Family caregivers
- Parents and grandparents

IDEA PAGES:

- **Infant Care:** A place to record observations and advice from caregivers. Include your observations on attachment and relationships, along with ideas for feeding, diapering, sleeping, and dressing.
- **Infant Activities:** Include developmentally appropriate activities you have observed. Include sensory, motor, music, and language activities.
- **Lullabies and Other Recordings for Babies:** List the recordings the children enjoyed.
- **Equipment and Toys for Infants:** What types of materials did you see the babies enjoying? Describe materials designed by teachers.
- **Toddler Care:** A place to record observations and advice from caregivers. Include tips on toilet learning, napping, eating, and self-help skills.

- **Toddler Behavior:** Include developmentally appropriate strategies used by caregivers to solve common problems such as fighting, biting, hitting, temper tantrums, and "NO!"
- **Toddler Activities, Songs, and Games:** Appropriate activities for this age group.
- **Books for Infants and Toddlers:** Write down those you want to remember.
- **Equipment and Toys for Toddlers:** What have you seen that works?
- **Relationships with Parents:** How do caregivers communicate to families?

Infant Care

Observation or Advice	Age
Example: Miss S, an occupational therapist, noted that during playtime, young babies should be put on their stomachs to help strengthen back muscles, encourage upper body strength, and encourage rolling over, creeping, and crawling. She noted that the recent pediatric recommendation of putting babies on their backs to sleep (to prevent SIDS) has caused a delay in these types of skills. She said that babies shouldn't be spending their waking hours on their backs!	2–6 months

Attachment between Caregiver and Child

Observation or Advice	Age
Example: The director of the infant program told me that they have a "primary caregiver" for each infant. This means that the same person will feed, rock, change, and play with the baby during his or her stay at the center. This is done to help the baby form a healthy attachment to one adult.	Birth to 12 months

Sensory Activities for Infants

Observation	Age
Example: Mrs. C created a touch blanket for babies. She sewed on patches of different types of materials, such as satin, fake fur, felt, burlap, and so on. Gently direct the child's attention to the different textures.	3–8 months

Motor Activities for Infants

Observation	Age
Example: The head teacher in the infant room pointed out that guidelines recommend that babies be placed on their backs for sleep. During the day, however, they should be placed on their stomachs to promote motor development. This week, she placed a four-month-old on his stomach and placed toys just a hair out of reach so he would stretch his arms to reach them.	4 months

Music Activities for Infants

Observation	Age
Example: The infants in Mrs. C's class love to feel rhythm with their bodies. To promote this, she often does "knee-bouncing songs." The teacher sits the child on her lap, facing eye to eye. She chants the rhyme while bouncing the child to the beat. The children she did this with really loved it and yelled "'gain, 'gain" (again) at the end! Chant: I have a little pony, his name is Macaroni. He trots and trots and then he stops! (Pause) My funny little pony, Macaroni. (Dip child backwards)	Must be able to support their head on their own. 9–10 months and older

Language Activities for Infants

Observation	Age
Example: Mrs. C pointed out some strategies I could use to promote infant language development. One strategy she often uses is restating and extending. For example, the child may only be able to say one word, like "ruck!". She restated his exclamation as follows: "Yes, look at the TRUCK—it's red and has a ladder and is really big!" She turned his one mispronounced word into a full sentence, allowing the child to hear and digest more vocabulary.	12–36 months

Lullabies and Other Recordings for Babies

Performer	Title	Description
Example: Hap Palmer	*Baby Songs* CD 1984 Educational Activities #B00004TVSG	A collection of upbeat songs that reflect babies' interests. Examples include: "Sitting in a High Chair," "My Mommy Comes Back," and "Daddy Be a Horsy."

Equipment and Toys for Infants

Description of Material	Purpose	Where to Purchase	Age
Example: "Winkle": Colorful loops made out of pliable plastic with a rattle inside.	The loops make it easy for a baby to grab with success. May be frozen for teething.	ABC School Supply 3312 N. Berkeley Lake Rd. Duluth, GA 30096 www.abcschoolsupply.com 1-800-669-4222	6–12 months

Toddler Care

Observation or Advice	Age
Example: Mrs. B noted that toddlers can be picky eaters. She recommended that teachers offer a variety of colors, textures, and flavors to encourage children to try different foods. She also recommended that toddlers be given choices to be sure they eat from all food groups. For example, offer saltines or graham crackers, or apple and pear slices. The child is empowered by the choice, but nutritional needs are still met.	1–2 years

Toddler Behavior

Observation or Advice	Age
Example: Every time I asked a toddler to do something, he replied, "NO!" Mrs. C recommended that I give him a choice to avoid "no" as an answer. For example: "Do you want to put away the block or the truck?" "No" is not an option. This really worked!	1–2 years

Toddler Activities, Songs, and Games

Observation	Age
Example: Ms. K put globs of shaving cream on the table. In one pile, she added a little blue tempera paint, in the other yellow. The children fingerpainted all over the table with this. Some of them were surprised to see the color green appear! The toddlers really enjoyed this sensory activity. Ms. K noted that this activity should only be done with direct adult supervision to be sure the children do not put the shaving cream in their mouths.	1–2 years

Books for Infants and Toddlers

Author	Title	Publisher/Date/ISBN	Description	Age
Example: Tom Arma	*Dress-Up Time!*	Grosset & Dunlap 1994 ISBN: 0448404389	Board book with photos of babies dressing up.	6–24 months

Equipment and Toys for Toddlers

Description of Material	Purpose	Where to Purchase	Age
Example: Small metal pails and a bag of wooden clothespins (not the kind that pinch!)	Toddlers love to put the clothespins in the pail, dump them out, and clip them on the edge of the pail. Encourages eye-hand coordination and concept of empty/full.	Supplies were purchased from a dollar store.	12–36 months

Teacher Resource Books: Infants and Toddlers

Title	Author	Publisher/Date/ISBN	Age	Notes
Example: *Infant and Toddler Experiences*	Fran Hast and Ann Hollyfield	Redleaf Press 1999 ISBN: 1884834574	Birth–3 years	This book is organized into experiences for infants and toddlers that include curiosity, connection, and coordination. Each experience includes materials needed and procedures to keep in mind.

Communicating with Parents

Observation or Advice	Age
Example: Miss B sends home a detailed form each day to communicate with the parents of her infants. She includes something special the child did that day, along with informational items such as number of feedings, diapering, times the child slept, and any milestones. She also includes a picture taken with an instant camera of the child each day to help the parents feel connected while they are at work.	Infants

CHAPTER 13

JOURNAL OF IDEAS
Behavior Strategies

WHO TO OBSERVE:

- Cooperating teachers
- Special education teachers
- Substitute teachers
- Parents

IDEA PAGES:

For Early Childhood Settings:

- **Indirect Guidance Strategies:** Teachers indirectly guide children's behavior by the behind-the-scenes work they do. Include room arrangements that were successful, schedules that worked, and material arrangements, including labeling of items, designated shelves, and distinct discovery centers.

- **Direct Guidance Strategies:** Teachers directly guide children's behavior with physical, verbal, and affective techniques. Include examples of guidance strategies you have observed in early childhood settings including transitions, meal-time strategies, and group-time strategies.

For Elementary School Settings:

- **Classroom Management Strategies:** As children move into elementary school, different classroom-management techniques are used. Give examples of successful positive reinforcement you have observed.

- **Attention Getters and Motivators:** Make note of how teachers bring the class to attention. How do they motivate the whole class to achieve good behavior?

- **Transition Strategies:** Moving from activity to activity or to a new classroom down the hall can be a time for potential problems. How do teachers help children make transitions smoothly between events or places?

- **Conflict-Management Strategies:** How do teachers help children solve their own problems? How do they calm down children who are upset?

Indirect Guidance Strategies

Observation	Age or Grade Level
Example: Free-play time is always calm in Mrs. B's preschool classroom. The room is clearly divided into interest centers, with the noisy areas away from the quiet areas. Every shelf is labeled with a photo or drawing of the toy that should be placed there. The block shelves have outlines of the different sizes of blocks on each shelf for easy clean-up. The children are well-behaved because they are busy and engaged in interesting activities. Clean-up is never a problem because of the labeling.	Ages 3–5

Successful Room Arrangements

Drawing of Floor Plan

Age or Grade Level _____

Drawing of Floor Plan

Age or Grade Level _____

Direct Guidance Strategies

Observation	Age or Grade Level
Example: Miss Sue had a biter in her toddler class. First, she or the assistant teacher observed the child and recorded her behavior and body language before she attempted to bite. The assistant shadowed her and physically guided her to a new location as soon as she showed signs of an impending bite. On the few occasions that she bit someone before being redirected, Miss Sue gave all of her attention to the victim rather than negative attention to the biter. "You hurt Sally," was what Miss Sue said to the biter. The biter helped administer first aid to the victim. After a month or so, the biting stopped. This combination of strategies worked.	Ages 1–2

Early Childhood Transition Strategies

Observation	Age or Grade Level
Example: When free-play time was coming to a close, Mrs. B would have a child helper play a rain stick to alert everyone that free play would be ending in five minutes (soon, in a child's mind). Once clean-up time began, she would put on the song, "Scat Like That" from the CD *On the Move* by Greg and Steve (Youngheart Records, 1998, #B00000DGMY). The children would sing along as they cleaned up the room. They knew that the room needed to be clean by the time the song ended. This really worked well!	Preschool

Early Childhood Mealtime Strategies

Observation	Age or Grade Level
Example: In Mrs. M's Head Start classroom, meals are always served family style. Two children set the tables, and the cook places bowls of food on the tables—for example, a bowl each of ziti, salad, cooked carrots, applesauce, and a pitcher of milk. A teacher sits at each table and eats lunch with the children, modeling manners and engaging in conversations. Children pass the bowls around the table, taking their own servings from each one. The center requires a "no, thank you" helping to encourage the children to try all foods. Children pour their own drinks using child-sized pitchers of milk. Meal time is calm and peaceful, since the children have responsibility for meeting their own needs. Hand washing always precedes lunchtime. Having a consistent routine also helps with behavior.	Preschool

Early Childhood Group-Time Strategies

Observation	Age or Grade Level
Example: Mrs. K pointed out some strategies she uses to keep good behavior during circle time. She always has the other adults spread out among the children in the circle, so that after every five children, there is an adult. This adult proximity helps to avoid problems.	Preschool

Elementary Classroom-Management Strategies

Observation	Age or Grade Level
Example: Mrs. M had pockets full of tickets. As children worked on their assignments, she walked around the room, observing. Children who were behaving were given tickets, as were children who responded with correct answers or made an effort to respond. The children kept little boxes in their desks to store their ticket collection. When they reached certain numbers, they were rewarded with special privileges, such as having lunch with the principal or a night with no homework. This immediate positive reinforcement really worked. There were very few behavior problems in this classroom.	Grades 2–5

Attention Getters

Observation	Age or Grade Level
Example: To bring the class back to attention, Mrs. G uses this little chant, saying the first two words of each line, with the children saying the last word. By the end of the chant, everyone is ready to listen. Teacher: Eyes are. . . . Children: watching! Teacher: Ears are. . . . Children: listening! Teacher: Feet are. . . . Children: sitting! Teacher: Hands are. . . . Children: still!	Grade 2

Elementary Class Motivators

Observation	Age or Grade Level
Example: During the winter, Mrs. R motivated her kindergarten class with a large picture of a snowperson. When the group was behaving nicely, a child could put a cotton ball on the snowperson. When the snowperson was filled in, the class would get an ice cream party.	K

Elementary Transition Strategies

Observation	Age or Grade Level
Example: Mrs. B believed that transitions should be opportunities for learning. When it was time for the children to move from circle time to centers, she made a guessing game out of each child's name. For example: "This person has three vowels in her name and three syllables! Her name starts with the same sound as K-K-K-Katie Kangaroo." She held up a card with a "K" on it. Catherine figured out it was her name and got up to go to her center. Mrs. B did this for each child. They really enjoyed it!	Grades K–2

Walking in the Halls

Observation	Age or Grade Level
Example: Ms. K sings a song with her first graders before they leave the classroom. It is sung to the tune of "Are You Sleeping?": Teacher: Are you ready? Children: Yes, we're ready! Teacher: For the hall? Children: For the hall! All: Quietly we'll tiptoe, voices will be very low, in the hall, in the hall. By the end of the song, the children are calm and ready to walk quietly.	Grades K–2

Conflict-Management Strategies

Observation	Age or Grade Level
Example: Mrs. B has a "Peace Table" in her kindergarten classroom. When children have a problem with each other, they have to go to the table and talk through the problem. Each child states his or her side of the issue and a compromise must be reached before the two children can return to play. This puts the responsibility on the children rather than on the teacher. If a problem can't be solved this way, the teacher will then intervene to help them work it through. Generally, this has worked for the children.	Grades K–2

Calming Upset Children

Observation	Age or Grade Level
Example: Mrs. B has many ideas for calming upset kindergartners. One idea is to fill an empty water bottle with colorful pom-poms, with one black pom-pom deep inside. The child has to try to get the black pom-pom out by using his pointer finger. This activity distracts the child from whatever was causing the problem. She finds it helpful in the first few days of school. Another thing she suggests is to fill a water bottle to the top with shampoo, super gluing the top on. The upset child turns the bottle over and waits for the giant bubble to come up from the bottom. It takes a full minute to happen! These two ideas definitely work!	Ages 2–5

Teacher Resource Books: Behavior Strategies

Title	Author	Publisher/Date/ISBN	Age or Grade Level	Notes
Example: *Meeting the Challenge: Effective Strategies for Challenging Behaviours in Early Childhood Environments*	B. Kaiser and J.S. Rasminsky	Canadian Child Care Federation 1999 ISBN: 0968515711	Ages 3–7	This book offers ideas and strategies to work with the most challenging behaviors and to help every child in your class.

CHAPTER 14

JOURNAL OF IDEAS
Working with Children with Special Needs

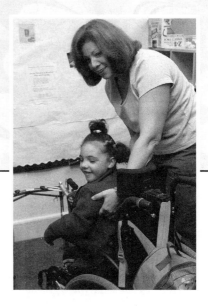

WHO TO OBSERVE:

- Cooperating teachers
- Assistants
- Special education teachers
- Music therapists
- Speech therapists
- Physical and occupational therapists

IDEA PAGES:

- **Behavior Strategies for Children with Special Needs:** Make note of how teachers adapt to the child's need.
- **IEPs:** Advice and examples.
- **Adaptation of Materials:** How have you seen teachers change materials to be better used by children?
- **Adaptation of Methodology:** What accommodations have you seen teachers make in their teaching methods?
- **Adaptation of Room Arrangement:** How have you seen classrooms made more accessible?

- **Sign Language:** Record words you have learned in the field here.
- **Differentiated Instruction:** How have teachers designed activities to meet the varying needs of their learners?
- **Assessment:** What signs and signals should the teacher look for to refer a child for evaluation?
- **Advice and Teacher Resources:** A place to record helpful teaching materials.

Behavior Strategies for Children with Special Needs

Observation or Advice	Age or Grade Level
Example: A child in Mrs. B's class demonstrated destructive behavior. He often hit other children or knocked down their blocks. He was very impulsive. The teacher responded to his frequent outbursts by putting him in time-out or telling him that what he did was wrong. However, this did not work. The psychologist recommended that she try to prevent the destructive behavior before it happened by paying attention to the child when he was not demanding it. "Catch him being good!" Mrs. B changed her techniques with this child by giving more attention to him when he was not being destructive and it worked! The number of destructive acts decreased significantly when she used this method.	All ages

IEPs—Individualized Education Plans

Observation or Advice	Notes
Example: Mrs. G shared a child's IEP with me. An IEP includes the following components: • Child's current level of performance • Annual general goal and two to four short-term objectives • Related service involvement and extent of participation in regular classes • Anticipated duration of services • Evaluation procedures, criteria, and schedules for measuring objectives She noted that progress reports for children with IEPs need to match the reporting schedule done for regular classes.	

Modification of Materials

Observation or Advice	Age or Grade Level
Example: Mrs. S created a vertical writing surface for a child with fine motor difficulties by mounting the back two legs of his desk to blocks that raised the back section higher than the front. The child demonstrated better control in writing after this adjustment.	Grades 1–2

Adaptation of Teaching Methods

Observation or Activity	Age or Grade Level
Example: Mrs. G noted the accommodations she gives for children with special needs in her second-grade class: • Allowing extended time to complete class work • Reading directions to the child • Giving the child additional time to process verbal and written information • Allowing the child to demonstrate what they've learned through a variety of means (oral, written, or as a project)	Primary grades

Modifications of Room Arrangements

Observation	Age or Grade Level
Example: Mrs. W rearranged her classroom to accommodate a child in a wheelchair. She created more open space for maneuverability and always had an open spot at tables used for centers. A larger-than-usual-size desk was brought in for this child's use. The higher level of the desktop accommodated the wheelchair nicely.	Primary grades

Sign Language

Drawings of sign language	Drawings of sign language

Differentiated Instruction

Observation or Activity	Age or Grade Level
Example: Mrs. G explained that differentiated instruction requires teachers to meet the needs of all learners—slow, typical, and fast learners. For example, when introducing an activity to her second-grade class, she will first present the activity to the whole class. Next, she will set up learning centers where she will have the directions written out in bold print for visual learners. Students who need reinforcement of the directions may have this need met individually at the center. At each center, she will have a rubric that offers the child a choice of level for completing the activity. For example, one level of the rubric may meet the needs of visual learners, another level may offer an oral report, and another may include movement, music, or drama.	Grades 1–3

Assessment

Observation of Assessment Tool or Advice	Age or Grade Level
Example: Miss S, the school occupational therapist, recommended that teachers refer children for services after observing several of these signs: • Avoids use of one body side • Changes crayon from hand to hand while coloring • Has difficulty cutting • Exhibits clumsy movements, trips, is "accident prone" • Has irregular or jerky eye movements • Reacts atypically to loud noises • Has difficulty with dressing tasks • Seems uncomfortable with (or avoids) sensory activities such as fingerpaints, feely boxes, clay, and sand	Preschool through primary grades

Children's Literature: Special Needs

Title	Author	Publisher/Date/ISBN	Age or Grade Level	Concepts
Example: *Someone Special Just Like You*	Tricia Brown and Fran Ortiz	Owlet 1995 ISBN: 0805042687	Preschool	A positive message that all children are lovable and worthwhile.

Teacher Resource Books: Special Needs

Title	Author	Publisher/Date/ISBN	Age or Grade Level	Notes
Example: *You Can Learn Sign Language!*	Jackie Kramer and Tali Ovadia	Troll Associates 2000 ISBN: 0816763364	All ages	A simple book that is useful for both children and adults. Easy-to-read illustrations teach the most common phrases needed.

CHAPTER 15

JOURNAL OF IDEAS
Teaching Materials

WHO TO OBSERVE:

- Cooperating teacher
- Assistants
- Special subject teachers
- Special education teachers

IDEA PAGES:

- **Bulletin-Board Ideas:** Draw or photograph bulletin boards you want to remember. Be sure to note bulletin boards you see in the halls or other classrooms.

- **Teaching Charts:** Draw or photograph the types of teaching charts you'd like to recreate for your own classroom.

- **Interactive Bulletin Boards:** Describe games that teachers have made for the children.

- **Felt-Board Materials:** Describe, draw, or photograph felt materials you have seen. Include the rhyme, finger play, or story that went with the prop.

- **Puppets:** Include glove puppets, stick puppets, and hand puppets that have worked well as motivators.

- **Teacher-Made Instruments:** Describe or photograph musical instruments made by teachers. Include a description of how to make it.

- **Motivating Props:** Describe props teachers have made to introduce lessons, such as feely bags or storytelling aprons.

- **Classroom-Management Materials:** Include pictorial schedules, attendance charts, job boards, and choice boards. Include your own creations as well.

- **Teacher Resource Books:** Include activity books, song books, curriculum materials, and other resources recommended to you by teachers.

- **Recommended Web Sites:** List addresses of helpful activity planning and other sites for teachers.

Bulletin-Board Ideas

Photo, Drawing, or Description	Age or Grade Level

Teaching Charts

Photo, Drawing, or Description	Age or Grade Level
Example: Mrs. M made this chart for her four-year-old class.	Ages 3–7

Autumn Leaves

Autumn leaves are
falling down, falling down
Autumn leaves are
falling down.
red
yellow
green
and
brown

Interactive Bulletin Boards

Photo, Drawing, or Description	**Age or Grade Level**
Matching pieces for this game are laminated and attached with Velcro®.	Ages 3–6

Shape match up game

heart · star · cresent · rectangle · triangle

diamond · oval · square · cross · circle

Felt-Board Props

Photo, Drawing, or Description	Rhyme, Finger Play, or Story	Age or Grade Level

Puppets

Photo, Drawing, or Description	Finger Play, Story, or Uses	Age or Grade Level

Teacher-Made Instruments

Photo, Drawing, or Description	How to Make	Age or Grade Level
	Example: Rain Stick Materials: Large, sturdy mailing tube 100–200 nails that are half the diameter of the tube Rice, tiny beads, gravel, or sand Hammer the nails into the tube to create an asterisk design inside. Fill the tube with rice and hot-glue the ends on. Cover the outside with decorated Con-Tact® paper to hide the nails. The nails should slow down the rice to create a rain-stick effect. If the rice travels too quickly, add more nails.	Ages 3–7

Motivating Props

Photo, Drawing, or Description	How Used	Age or Grade Level
Example: Mrs. B used a "feely bag" to introduce her new theme. Inside the bag was a small pumpkin. The children passed around the bag and tried to guess what was inside by feeling the shape from the outside. After everyone had a chance to guess, she opened the bag and allowed the children to touch the pumpkin.	The feely bag really excited the children and motivated them to come to circle time.	Preschool

Management Props: Pictorial Schedules

Photo, Drawing, or Description	How Used	Age or Grade Level
Example: Miss Tricia made drawings of daily events such as story, play time, circle, snack, hand washing, toileting, outdoor play, and so on. She attached them all to a large strip of Velcro®. As each part of the day was completed, a child would go to the schedule, remove the card for the activity just completed, and place the next event in the top spot. This worked very well.	She used this to help children sequence the day.	Preschool–kindergarten

Management Props: Attendance Charts

Photo, Drawing, or Description	How Used	Age or Grade Level
Example: Mrs. W created an attendance board with small hooks. She made a small, laminated card with each child's first name and attached each card to a hook. When the children arrived at school each day, they took their name off the hook and put it in a basket. Two months later, she put up only their last names, which helped them learn to read their own names. Two months later, they had to find their phone number. Two months after that, they found their street address.	Mrs. W's class learned their first names, last names, phone numbers, and addresses over the year through this simple attendance chart! The teacher could also immediately see who was absent!	K

Management Props: Job Boards

Photo, Drawing, or Description	Age or Grade Level
Example: Mrs. L used library-card pockets covered with pictures of the class jobs, including fish feeders, line leaders, line cabooses, teacher helpers, table setters, and so on. In each pocket, she placed a tongue depressor with a photo of a child glued to the top. The children were able to "read" the pictures to find out what their jobs were.	Preschool through early elementary

Management Props: Choice Boards

Photo, Drawing, or Description	Age or Grade Level
Example: Miss T placed strips of Velcro® on the wall next to each interest center. If three children fit in that area, there were three pieces of Velcro®. She took photos of each child, laminated them, and attached Velcro® on the back. The child placed his or her photo on the strip in the center where they planned to play.	Preschool through elementary

Teacher Resource Books: Teaching Materials

Title	Author	Publisher/Date/ISBN	Age or Grade Level	Content Summary
Example: *Sing Me A Story! Tell Me A Song!: Creative Curriculum Activities for Teachers of Young Children*	Hilda L. Jackman	Corwin Press 1999 ISBN: 0803967977	Preschool through elementary	An excellent collection of thematic units, including fall, winter, spring, summer, and colors. Each unit includes activity ideas for art, music, movement, science, math, motor skills, cooking, and stories.

Web Sites for Teachers

Web Site Address	Summary of Content
Example: National Association for the Education of Young Children http://www.naeyc.org	A comprehensive site that includes information about professional development, conferences, public policy, and accreditation. It also includes information for families and teacher resources.

CHAPTER 16

JOURNAL OF IDEAS

Working with Parents

WHO TO OBSERVE:

- Cooperating teachers
- Assistants
- Directors/principals
- Special educators
- Support staff

IDEA PAGES:

- **Parent Communications:** Collect samples or describe parent newsletters, parent bulletin boards, or other methods you have seen teachers use to communicate with parents.
- **Parent-Teacher Conferences:** Describe the process you have observed. Any advice from cooperating teachers about successful conferences?
- **Problem Solving:** Describe any advice about solving conflicts with parents.

- **Open House Ideas:** If you attend a school open house, describe how your cooperating teacher presented the program to parents.
- **Progress Reports:** Collect samples or outline written reports describing children's progress. Any advice about how to complete these forms?
- **Special Events for Families:** Describe any special events planned for parents and children.
- **Parents as Volunteers:** Describe how parents were involved in the classroom. How were parents made to feel welcome?

Parent Communications

Description	Age or Grade Level
Example: Mrs. K sends home a class newsletter every Friday. The newsletter includes a report of what the children worked on that week, suggested questions the parent could ask their child, and plans for the next week. The newsletter also serves as a way to request volunteer help for centers, field trips, and fund-raisers.	All ages

Parent-Teacher Conferences

Observation or Advice	Age or Grade Level
Example: Mrs. F allowed me to sit in on a conference. I noted that she began by making the parents feel welcome. She had coffee available and gave a brief tour of the classroom, showing the parents their child's desk and displayed work. She started the conference by telling the parents about the positive progress their child had made. She showed examples of the child's work throughout. She then discussed areas of needed work and set up a plan for improvement that would involve the parents. She made sure to end the conference on a positive note and encouraged the adults to contact her with any questions. This format worked very well in helping the parents become partners in their child's education.	All ages

Problem Solving with Parents

Observation or Advice	Age or Grade Level
Example: Mrs. B was concerned about the behavior problems of a boy in her preschool class. Every morning around 10:00 he would become fussy and often acted out, sometimes hitting other children. She noted that after snack, at 10:30, his behavior returned to normal. She contacted the parents to discuss the problem and found out that the child was not getting breakfast at home before coming to school. His behavior was a result of hunger. The parents were very stressed about getting him to eat in the morning as they all rushed out to work. Together, Mrs. B and the parents devised a plan for the child to eat a breakfast snack when he arrived at school. For the short term, this solved the problem.	All ages

Open-House Ideas

Observation or Description	Age or Grade Level
Example: Mrs. B felt the need to defend play at her nursery school. The parents were implying that child's play was a waste of time and that she should be spending more time with direct teaching! To educate the parents, she developed a slide show with photos taken of the current class at play. As she showed the slides, she explained what concepts the children were learning through their manipulation of materials. When the parents saw their own children in the slides classifying, counting, creating letters out of dough, balancing, singing, dancing, and reading stories, they backed off on pressuring Mrs. B about direct teaching. After the show, the parents visited the classroom, where Mrs. B had put signs over each learning area to explain what the children learn while playing. Parents were also encouraged to participate in an open-ended art activity, such as marble rolling. The night was a success!	All ages

Progress Reports

Sample, Description, or Advice	Age or Grade Level

Special Events for Families

Observation or Description	Age or Grade Level
Example: All of the kindergarten, first-, and second-grade classes held a "Walk About" night. It was held in the middle of the year, long after Open House. Parents, family members, and the children were invited. Each class had all of the children's work on display. Special foods were available in each room. One room had storytelling sessions, another had art activities, another had science experiments, and another had math games. It was a wonderful way for children to show their families what their school day was like.	K–2

Parents as Volunteers

Observation or Advice	Age or Grade Level
Example: Mrs. A welcomed parent volunteers into her classroom. To make this partnership successful, she always had a plan of action for the parents in her room. Parents monitored centers, read stories, and worked with individual children. Mrs. A did not encourage parents to pop in. She would send home sign-up sheets each week with her weekly newsletter. The sign-ups gave the times and volunteer "duty" that was needed. Working parents (who often feel left out) were welcome to assist at home by cutting out bulletin-board shapes and letters and by typing words for the children's books for illustration and "publication." (The school had an annual author's fair to celebrate the children's writing.) This system worked well.	Preschool through primary grades

Journal of Reflection

CHAPTER 17

JOURNAL OF REFLECTION
Becoming a Reflective Teacher

IN THIS CHAPTER

- Reflection defined
- Steps to becoming reflective
- Reflection pages

WHAT IS REFLECTION?

Reflective thinking has long been recognized as a factor in improving the quality of teaching. McAllister and Neubert (1995) defined reflection as a type of critical thinking that engaged teachers in examining and raising questions about their teaching. Dewey (1933) viewed reflection as a cycle that stemmed from the doubt and confusion felt in an experience that led to purposeful inquiry and a resolution of the problem. To reflect, teachers must question what, why, and how they do things.

STEPS TO BECOMING REFLECTIVE

Beginning teachers begin to develop reflection by first observing more experienced teachers and analyzing their successes. The first half of this book was designed to help you complete this step. As you observed and analyzed other people's teaching, you were in effect developing your own philosophy about how you think things should be done. Think about it. Why did you choose the examples you recorded on the Idea Pages? You probably chose those examples because they were activities or strategies you agreed or felt comfortable with.

To improve your own teaching, you need to begin to question what, why, and how you do things. The reflection journal pages will guide you in a self-dialogue where you can critically think about your practice with children.

This chapter has been set up to give you some practice with becoming reflective. Many teachers keep journals, but more often than not, these become diaries that simply record events. In a reflection journal, the writer questions events, has a self-dialogue analyzing the questions and answers, and concludes with an attempt at solving problems for future use.

HOW TO COMPLETE A REFLECTION ENTRY

- **Activity Summary:** Start by summarizing the event. This is your "diary" entry where you record what happened. Try to include as much detail as possible and note children's responses, both positive and negative.

- **Questions To Ask:** Review the summary and write several questions you have about the event. This is where you use those "how, what, and why" types of questions. Think about what your expectation for the activity was and what actually happened. Ask yourself why?

- **Reflective Thoughts:** In this section, try to answer those questions. This is where you analyze your activity, and try to figure out what went wrong or why something worked so well. Think of this section as "talking out loud."

- **Decision Making:** Finally, after summarizing, inquiring, and analyzing your activity, you will come to some decisions about changes you want to make. How will you implement that lesson differently next time? How will you meet the needs of all the children in your class? How can you apply what you learned from the experience?

These pages are designed to help you become comfortable with the process of reflecting. An example is included to get you started. When you feel confident with this process, you will be ready to move onto Chapter 18 where you can reflect about your teaching experiences on a regular basis. Chapter 19 will help you summarize your thoughts, develop your philosophy, note favorite activities, and chronicle your successes and failures. Visit these pages often to update your ideas and to see how much you have grown professionally.

REFERENCES

Dewey, J. (1933). *How we think.* Chicago: Henry Regnery.

McAllister, E. A., & Neubert, G. A. (1995). *New teachers helping new teachers: Preservice peer coaching.* Bloomington, IN: EDINFO Press.

Becoming Reflective: An Example

Activity Objective: The children will create a cloud picture and complete the sentence, "It looked like a cloud, but it was a _____."

Activity Summary: I read the book *It Looked Like Spilt Milk* during circle time. The children seemed very interested. After the story, I explained the follow-up activity, which was for each child to make their own "spilt milk" picture by painting with a mixture of one-half shaving cream and one-half glue. (When dry, it puffs up like a cloud.) I showed them the one I made, which was a picture of a cat. On the bottom of the page, I directed the children to read along the fill-in line, "It looked like a cloud, but it was a ___." The children helped me spell the word "cat." I dismissed each group to go to their table to begin. They were all excited about the mixture. I had wanted them to use paintbrushes, but many stuck their hands in it and fingerpainted. I had to constantly remind them to fluff up the paint, since some were smearing it. As I circulated around the tables, I realized that at least half the class was making cats. At that point, I tried to get them to come up with different ideas for shapes for their clouds. The lesson took much longer than I thought. We had to stop before completing the pictures to go to music. By the time we got back, what they had done had dried, so it was impossible to finish. Some children simply made clouds, and had a difficult time filling in the sentence since the picture was supposed to be of an identifiable shape. I was very unhappy with the outcome and my objectives were not met.

Questions to Ask:

1. Why did more than half the class make cats or simply clouds?
2. Why did they all try to fingerpaint with the mixture?
3. Why did we run out of time?
4. Why did the children have trouble filling in the sentence?
5. Why were they so attentive to the story?

Reflective Thoughts: I realize that I should not have shown the model of a cat, since many of the children simply copied my idea. I should have helped them brainstorm new ideas before we jumped right into the art project. The children in this classroom are used to doing work sheets most of the time. I think they were so excited to experiment with the paint that the whole point of making the pictures was lost. I could see that the children were really enjoying the sensory experience. Maybe I should have just let them experiment instead of insisting on the outcome. I definitely need to work on budgeting my time. I should have allowed more than 10 minutes to have them complete the project. Perhaps this would have been better as a center rather than a whole-group project. Then there would have been more time, less stress, and I would have been able to work with a smaller group of children, which I'm more comfortable with anyway. I think I need to give clearer directions, too. I didn't make it clear that they needed to use the paintbrushes and I didn't help them come up with cloud-shape ideas until it was too late. I am pleased with the way I read the story. I used a lot of inflection and involved the children in guessing the words on each page. The children were very well-behaved and participated very well. I didn't realize until now how important it is to use my voice effectively. So at least I know that they got the idea of the story!

(continued)

Decision Making: I learned many things from this activity. The next time I present this story/activity, I will not use a model. Children want to conform to teachers' expectations and so they all copied mine. I will also add time to the circle-time portion for brainstorming. The children clearly needed help coming up with ideas. I will also offer the shaving cream/glue mixture as a sensory activity BEFORE I ever do it as a product-oriented project like this. I think if the children had prior experience with the mixture, they wouldn't have spent so much time exploring it. I also think this activity would be more appropriate for an older group of children. Next time I present this, it will be to first graders rather than young kindergartners. This group didn't even know all their letters yet. My expectation of writing a word in the sentence was too high. I will also make a point of writing on a cue card the directions I plan to give to the children. I tend to ad-lib too much. It's clear I need the steps written ahead of time.

Becoming Reflective

Date _____

Activity Objective:

Activity Summary:

Questions to Ask:

1.

2.

3.

4.

5.

Reflective Thoughts:

Decision Making:

CHAPTER 18

JOURNAL OF REFLECTION
Journal

IN THIS CHAPTER:

Reflection Pages

SUGGESTIONS FOR REFLECTING:

- Take the time to think.
- Schedule time to reflect.
- Pretend you are writing to a friend or family member.
- Start with small goals.
- Jot down thoughts when you have them; reflect later.
- Refer to your own beliefs and values.
- Keep an open mind—try something new.
- Ask for others' opinions and ideas.
- Ask questions: How, What, Why?
- Find answers to your questions.
- Inquire.
- Look for and resolve problems.
- Make and implement decisions.

Date:

PART II • Journal of Reflection

Date:

Date:

PART II • Journal of Reflection

Date:

Date:

Date:

Date:

Date:

Date:

Date:

CHAPTER 19

JOURNAL OF REFLECTION

Developing a Teaching Philosophy

IN THIS CHAPTER

- Philosophy
- My best activities
- Thoughts about children
- Successes and failures
- Conferencing notes

REFLECTION PAGES:

- **Philosophy:** Reflection pages will guide you to review others' teaching in a reflective way. Look at the best and worst lessons and question why they succeeded or failed. You can use this same approach with your own lessons when you begin teaching. Begin to think about your philosophy of teaching—how you think children learn, what theorists you align yourself with, and how you would do things differently in your own classroom.

- **My Best Activities:** Here's a place to record your own activities for future reference.

- **Thoughts about Children:** The more you work with children, the more you can make sense of child development. Here's a place to record your thoughts about child development based on your experiences.

- **Successes and Failures:** A place to record your proudest and most difficult experiences. Be sure to date these so that in the future you can see how you have grown as a teacher.

- **Conference Notes:** A place to record conferences with your cooperating teacher, your college supervisor, and/or your mentors.

Developing My Teaching Philosophy

Analyze the best activities I've observed other teachers implementing . . .

Date	Activity, Thoughts, and Questions

Developing My Teaching Philosophy

How I would change an activity that I've observed others lead . . .

Date	Activity, Thoughts, and Questions

Developing My Teaching Philosophy

I believe children learn best by . . .

Date	Thoughts

Developing My Teaching Philosophy

Theorists/educators I most align myself with . . .

Date	Thoughts

Developing My Teaching Philosophy

If the student teaching placement was my own classroom, I would . . .

Date	Thoughts

Developing My Teaching Philosophy

My thoughts on guidance and classroom management . . .

Date	Thoughts

My Best Activities, Lessons, and/or Centers

Date	Description of Activity	Reactions of Children

Need extra forms? Download this page at http://www.earlychilded.delmar.com

Thoughts about Children:

Date	Thought or Observation
Example: 4/8/03	I'm beginning to understand how young children have not yet developed the concept of conservation. It never made that much sense in the textbook, yet today I saw it in action! At snack time, the children had graham crackers and juice. Mary and Tom got into a big argument over who had more. Each child was given one large cracker. Tom took his large cracker and broke it into four pieces. Mary did not see him do this, but was furious that he got four crackers and she could only have one. I tried to show her that she also had four "little" crackers in her big cracker by lining up the four little ones against the big one. She would hear nothing of it! As far as she was concerned, Tom had more because it looked like more on his dish. The next time, I'll suggest that the teacher break up all of the big graham crackers!

My Teaching

Date	Thought
I was most proud when . . .	

My Teaching

I was surprised when . . .

Date	Thought

My Teaching

I was excited when . . .	
Date	**Thought**

My Teaching

I was disappointed when . . .	
Date	**Thought**

My Teaching

I was upset when . . .

Date	Thought

My Teaching

I felt like screaming when . . .

Date	Thought

My Teaching

I wish I had . . .

Date	Thought

Goals

	When I get my own classroom, I want to . . .	
Date	**Thought**	

Goals

Things I'd like to learn more about

Date	Thought

Notes of Conferences with Cooperating Teacher, Supervisor, or Mentor

Date	Discussion	Goals

Need extra forms? Download this page at http://www.earlychilded.delmar.com

CHAPTER 20

JOURNAL OF REFLECTION
Professional Development

IN THIS CHAPTER:

- School structure
- Faculty meetings
- Committee meetings
- Communications
- Ethical issues
- Advocacy
- Your professional growth and plans

REFLECTION PAGES:

- **School Structure:** Reflect about the different schools you have visited, interned at, and worked in. Make note of the political structure, organization, and teams.
- **Faculty Meetings:** Reflect about your experiences attending and participating in faculty meetings.
- **Committee Meetings:** Reflect about your experiences at school committee meetings. Describe the committee, the members, and the work of the group.
- **Communications:** Reflect about the communication structure of the school. Include examples of school newsletters, the e-mail system, and Web pages.

- **Ethical Issues:** Reflect about any issues you encountered during your student teaching and first paid positions.
- **Advocacy:** Include any work you complete on behalf of children and families. Include volunteer work with advocacy organizations.
- **Videography:** List teaching videos you'd like to remember for future study, research, or training opportunities.
- **Professional Development:** Record courses completed, conferences and seminars attended, and memberships in professional organizations. Include references.
- **Goals:** A place to think about the future.

School Structure

Name of School	Administration	Faculty/Staff	Staff/Child Ratios	Notes

Faculty/Staff Meetings

Date and School	Agenda/Discussion	Reflection

Committee Meetings

Date/School	Committee Agenda	Reflections

Communications

Date/School	Example of Communication	Notes

Ethical Issues

Date	Issue	Reflection

Advocacy—Volunteer Work

Dates	Organization Volunteered For	Description of Work

Videography

Topics	Title of Video	Producer	Summary
Example: Integrated curriculum	*Teaching the Whole Child in the Kindergarten*	NAEYC 1509 16th St., NW Washington, DC 20036 1-800-424-2460 www.naeyc.org	This video shows how two kindergarten classes in Hawaii integrate the curriculum areas through center-based activities.

Courses Completed

Date Completed	Course Number and College	Course Name	Credits Earned	Grade Received

Conferences and Seminars Attended

Dates	Seminar or Workshop Title	Sponsoring Organization	Hours Attended	CEU or Professional Development Credits

Professional Organization Membership(s)

Date of Membership	Organization	Address/ Phone Number/ Web Site	Involvement (Officer, committee work, workshops, meetings)

References I Can Use When Applying for a Position

Name of Teacher/Administrator	School and Address	Phone/E-mail

Goals—Professional Development Plans

Certificates and Degrees Earned

Name of Certificate or Degree Earned	College or University	Credits	Date Earned

Honors and Awards

Date	Honor or Award	Presented By

Index

A

Activities, recording of best, 204, 205–211
Adaptation of materials
  idea pages, 151
Adaptation of methodology
  idea pages, 151
  observed activities, 155
Adaptation of room arrangements
  idea pages, 151
  observed activities, 156
Adding
  idea pages, 74
  observed activities, 87
Advice and teacher resources, 151
Advocacy, reflection on, 223, 229
Alphabet
  idea pages, 23
  K-2 teaching strategies, 29
Art, 3–12
Art displays
  idea pages, 3
  observed activities, 9
Art-materials
  recipes, 3, 6
  supply list, 8
Art projects
  idea pages, 3
  observed activities, 5
Art resource books, 11
Art teachers, observation of, 3
Art therapists, observation of, 3
Assessment
  idea pages, 151
  observed activities, 159
Assistants, observation of
  art, 3
  children with special needs, working
    with, 151
  cooking and nutrition, 64
  integrated curriculum, 101
  language arts, 23
  motor development, 92
  music and movement, 13
  observation and assessment, 108
  social studies, 36
  teaching materials, 162
  working with parents, 176

Attendance charts, 162, 171
Attention getters and motivators
  idea pages, 136
  observed activities, 144, 145
Author studies
  idea pages, 23
  observed activities, 33
Awards, 237

B

Basic first aid and infant/child CPR, notes to
  remember for, 117
Becoming reflective
  example, 189–190
  journal pages, 191–192
Behavior strategies, 136–150
  children with special needs, for, 151, 152
  early childhood settings, 136
  elementary school settings, 136
  ideas, 136
  resource books, 150
Block play, 81
Books
  children's. See Children's literature
  infants and toddlers, for, 120, 132
  teachers, for. See Teacher resource books
Brainstorming, 101, 102
Bulletin-board ideas, 162, 163

C

Calendar activities and routines for K-2
  idea pages, 74
  observed activities, 84
Calming upset children, 149
Cardinal numbers, 75
Case studies, 108, 110
Certificates earned, 236
Children
  calming upset, 149
  thoughts about, recording, 204, 212
Children's artwork, ideas for displaying, 9
Children's literature
  art, 10
  art concepts, with, 3
  cooking and nutrition, 71–72
  health and safety, 111, 118

  language arts, 23, 25
  math concepts, with, 74, 90
  music and movement, 13, 21
  science concepts, 57
  social studies, 36, 46
  special needs children, 160
Children with special needs, working with,
    151–161
  ideas, 151
Children with special needs resource
    books, 161
Choice boards, 162, 173
Classification and seriation (order)
  activities, 78
Class pets
  idea pages, 48
  observed activities, 55
Classroom-management materials, 162
Classroom management strategies
  idea pages, 136
  observed activities, 143
Committee meetings, reflection on, 223,
    226
Common childhood illnesses and allergies
  idea pages, 111
  observed activities, 116
Communicating with parents
  example, 177
  idea pages, 176
  infants and toddlers, of, 135
Communications, reflection on, 223, 227
Computers, 61
Computer software, 62
Concept web
  example, 102
  form, 103
Conference notes, recording of, 204, 222
Conferences and seminars attended,
    recording of, 232
Conflict-management strategies
  idea pages, 136
  observed activities, 148
Cookbooks for children, 72
Cooking and nutrition, 64–73
  ideas, 64
Cooking and nutrition resource books, 64, 73
Cooperating teachers, notes on conferences
    with, 222

Cooperating teachers, observation of
    art, 3
    behavior strategies, 136
    children with special needs, working
        with, 151
    cooking and nutrition, 64
    health and safety, 111
    infants and toddlers, 120
    integrated curriculum, 101
    language arts, 23
    math, 74
    motor development, 92
    music and movement, 13
    observation and assessment, 108
    science, 48
    social studies, 36
    teaching materials, 162
    working with parents, 176
Counting, 75
Courses completed, recording of, 231
CPR, notes to remember for, 117
Creative art activities
    idea pages, 3
    observed activities, 4
Creative drama
    idea pages, 23
    observed activities, 24
Creative movement activities, 13, 16
Cultural activities
    idea pages, 36
    observed activities, 38

D
Degrees earned, 236
Developmentally appropriate holiday
        activities
    idea pages, 36
    observed activities, 39
Development of teaching philosophy,
        204–222
Differentiated instruction
    idea pages, 151
    observed activities, 158
Direct guidance strategies
    idea pages, 136
    observed activities, 139
Directors and principals, observation of
    health and safety, 111
    working with parents, 176
Discovery centers
    idea pages, 48
    observed activities, 49
Dramatic play prop boxes
    idea pages, 36
    observed activities, 43

E
Early childhood
    group-time strategies, 136, 142
    mealtime strategies, 136, 141
    transition strategies, 136, 140
Elementary transition strategies
    idea pages, 136
    observed activities, 146
Emergency procedures
    idea pages, 111
    observed activities, 114

Emergent literacy in early childhood
    idea pages, 23
    observed activities, 26
Equipment and toys
    infants, for, 120, 128
    toddlers, for, 120, 133
Ethical issues, reflection on, 223, 228
Experiments
    idea pages, 48
    observed activities, 52

F
Faculty meetings, reflection on, 223, 225
Families, special events for
    idea pages, 176
    observed activities, 182
Family caregivers, observation of infants and
        toddlers, 120, 122
Favorite poems, 28
Felt-board materials, 162, 166
Field trips
    idea pages, 36
    observed activities, 41
Fine motor development, activities for
    idea pages, 92
    observed activities, 93
    writing, 94
Finger plays, music and movement, 13, 14
Fire safety
    idea pages, 111
    observed activities, 113
First aid and infant/child CPR, notes to
        remember for, 117

G
Geography and mapping, teaching
        activities, 44
    idea pages, 36
Goals, recording of, 220–221, 223, 235
Grandparents, observation of
    infants and toddlers, 120
    social studies, 36
Graphing activities
    idea pages, 74
    observed activities, 82
Gross motor development, activities for
    idea pages, 92
    observed activities, 95
Group-time strategies, early childhood
    idea pages, 136
    observed activities, 142
Guest artists/visitors, music and movement, 13
Guest speakers, observation of, 36, 42
Guidance strategies
    direct, 136, 139
    indirect, 136, 137

H
Halls, walking in the, 147
Health and safety, 111–119
    activities, 111, 112
    ideas, 111
    resource books, 119
Healthy snacks
    idea pages, 64
    observed activities, 70

Historical events in primary grades, teaching
        activities, 45
    idea pages, 36
Holiday activities, developmentally
        appropriate
    idea pages, 36
    observed activities, 39
Home and community activities/centers, 40
Honors and awards, 237

I
IEPs
    idea pages, 151
    observed activities, 153
Illnesses and allergies, common childhood
    idea pages, 111
    observed activities, 116
Indirect guidance strategies
    idea pages, 136
    observed activities, 137
Individualized Education Plans (IEPs)
    idea pages, 151
    observed activities, 153
Infant activities
    idea pages, 120
    language activities, 126
    motor activities, 124
    music activities, 125
    sensory activities, 123
Infant care
    idea pages, 120
    observed activities, 121
Infants and toddlers, 120–135
    books for, 120, 132
    ideas, 120
    resource books, 134
Instruments, music and movement, 13, 20
Integrated curriculum, 101–107
    ideas, 101
    resource books, 101, 107
Interactive bulletin boards
    example, 165
    idea pages, 162
Invention centers
    idea pages, 48
    observed activities, 56
Investigations
    conducted by children, 51
    idea pages, 48

J
Job boards, 162, 172
Journal, reflection, 193–203

K
Keeping children safe and healthy, proce-
        dures for
    idea pages, 111
    observed activities, 115

L
Language activities for infants, 126
Language arts, 23–35
    ideas, 23
    resource books, 34

Lullabies and other recordings for babies
idea pages, 120
observed activities, 127

M

Management props
attendance charts, 171
choice boards, 162, 173
idea pages, 162
job boards, 162, 172
pictorial schedules, 170
Mapping, teaching
activities, 44
idea pages, 36
Materials, adaptation of
idea pages, 151
observed activities, 154
Math, 74–91
ideas, 74
Math concept development
idea pages, 74
observed activities, 75
Math games and materials
idea pages, 74
observed activities, 89
Math resource books, 91
Math resource teachers, observation
of, 74
Mealtime strategies, early childhood
idea pages, 136
observed activities, 141
Meetings, reflections on
committee, 223, 226
faculty, 223, 225
Mentors, notes on conferences with,
222
Methodology, adaptation of
idea pages, 151
observed activities, 155
Modification of materials
idea pages, 151
observed activities, 154
Modification of room arrangements
idea pages, 151
observed activities, 156
Money concepts, 83
Motivating props
example, 169
idea pages, 162
Motivators
idea pages, 136
observed activities, 145
Motor activities for infants, 124
Motor development, 92–100
ideas, 92
resource books, 100
Movement with props, 13, 17
Music activities for infants, 125
Music and movement, 13–22
ideas, 13
resource books, 13, 22
Music interest centers
center or activity, 19
idea pages, 13
Music teachers and therapists, observation
of children with special needs, working
with, 151
music and movement, 13

N

Nature activities
idea pages, 48
observed activities, 53
Nature guides/rangers, observation of, 48
Numerals, 75
Nutritional activities
idea pages, 64
observed activities, 69
Nutrition ideas, 64
Nutritionist, observation of, 64

O

Observation and assessment, 108–110
case studies, 108, 110
ideas, 108
observation methods, 108, 109
Occupational therapists, observation of
children with special needs, working with,
151
motor development, 92
One-cup cooking ideas
idea pages, 64
observed activities, 65–66
100th day of school
idea pages, 74
observed activities, 85
Open house ideas, 176, 180
Ordinal numbers (first, second, third), 76
Outdoor play equipment
idea pages, 92
observed activities, 99
Outdoor sandbox play, 98
Outdoor water play
idea pages, 92
observed activities, 97

P

Parent communications. See Communicating
with parents
Parents, observation of
behavior strategies, 136
communications with parents, 135
infants and toddlers, 120
relationships with infants and toddlers,
120
social studies, 36
Parents, working with, 176–183
ideas, 176
Parents as volunteers
idea pages, 176
observed activities, 183
Parent-teacher conferences
idea pages, 176
observed activities, 178
Patterning
idea pages, 74
observed activities, 80
Philosophy, development of teaching,
204–222
Physical education teachers, observation of,
92
Physical therapists, observation of
children with special needs, working with,
151
motor development, 92

Pictorial schedules, 162, 170
Place value
idea pages, 74
observed activities, 88
Playground play
idea pages, 92
observed activities, 96
Poetry
favorite poems, 28
observed activities, 27
Principals, observation of
health and safety, 111
working with parents, 176
Problem-solving ideas for working with
parents, 176, 179
Procedures for keeping children safe
and healthy
idea pages, 111
observed activities, 115
Professional development, 223–237
Professional memberships, 233
Professional references, 234
Progress reports, 176, 181
Project approach
form, 106
idea pages, 101
Prop boxes, dramatic play
idea pages, 36
observed activities, 43
Props
management. See Management props
motivating, 162, 169
movement with, 13, 17
Psychologists, observation of, 108
Puppets, 162, 167

R

Reading teachers
K-2, advice for, 23, 35
observation of, 23, 108
Recipes for art-materials
idea pages, 3
observed activities, 6
Recipes for cooking, 65–68
Recipes for science materials
idea pages, 48
observed activities, 54
Recordings, music and movement, 13, 18
Recreational therapists, observation of, 92
References, recording of, 234
Reflection
defined, 187
suggestions for, 193
Reflection journal, 193–203
Reflection pages, 204
Reflective teacher
becoming, steps to, 187–188
journal, 193–203
reflection entry
example, 189–190
how to complete, 188
reflection pages, 191–192
Relationships with parents, 120
Resource books for teachers. See Teacher
resource books
Room arrangements
adaptation of, 151, 156
successful, 138

S

Safety issues
  art, 12
  health and safety. See Health and safety
Safety officers (fire, police), observation of, 111
Sandbox play, 98
School cook, observation of, 64
School nurse, observation of, 111
School structure, reflection on, 223, 224
Science, 48–63
  ideas, 48
Science books, 48
Science centers
  idea pages, 48
  observed activities, 49
Science material recipes
  idea pages, 48
  observed activities, 54
Science materials to find or purchase
  idea pages, 48
  observed activities, 60
Science museum staff, observation of, 48
Science projects and science fair ideas for elementary age children
  idea pages, 48
  observed activities, 58
Science resource books, 63
Scientific method, observation of, 59
Self and family, activities about
  idea pages, 36
  observed activities, 37
Seminars attended, recording of, 232
Sensory activities for infants, 123
Shape and form, 77
Sight words and word-wall ideas, 31
Sign language, 151, 157
Size and measurement, 79
Social studies, 36–47
  ideas, 36
  resource books, 47
Social workers, observation of, 108
Songs
  idea pages, 13
  observed activities, 15
Special education teachers, observation of
  behavior strategies, 136
  children with special needs, working with, 151
  integrated curriculum, 101
  language arts, 23
  math, 74
  motor development, 92
  observation and assessment, 108
  science, 48
  social studies, 36
  teaching materials, 162
  working with parents, 176
Special events for families
  idea pages, 176
  observed activities, 182
Special subject teachers, observation of
  integrated curriculum, 101
  teaching materials, 162

Speech therapists, observation of
  children with special needs, working with, 151
  language arts, 23
Spelling and word games
  idea pages, 23
  observed activities, 30
Staff members, observation of
  art, 3
  music and movement, 13
Steps to becoming reflective, 187–188
Substitute teachers, observation of, 136
Subtracting
  idea pages, 74
  observed activities, 87
Successes and failures, recording of, 204, 213–219
Successful room arrangements, 138
Supervisors, notes on conferences with, 222
Supplies, art, 3, 7
Support staff, observation of, 176

T

Teacher-made instruments
  example, 168
  idea pages, 162
Teacher resource books
  art, 11
  behavior strategies, 150
  children with special needs, 161
  cooking and nutrition, 64, 73
  health and safety, 119
  infants and toddlers, 134
  integrated curriculum, 101, 107
  language arts, 34
  math, 91
  motor development, 100
  music and movement, 13, 22
  science, 63
  social studies, 47
  teaching materials, 162, 174
  themes, units, and projects, 107
Teaching charts
  example, 164
  idea pages, 162
Teaching historical events in primary grades
  activities, 45
  idea pages, 36
Teaching materials, 162–175
  ideas, 162
  resource books, 162, 174
Teaching methods, adaptation of
  idea pages, 151
  observed activities, 155
Teaching philosophy, development of, 204–222
Technology in classroom, use of
  idea pages, 48
  observed activities, 61
Telling time
  idea pages, 74
  observed activities, 86
Themes, units, and projects resource books, 107

Themes or units
  example, 104
  form, 105
  idea pages, 101
Therapists, observation of, 92, 108
Thoughts about children, 204, 212
Toddler activities, songs and games
  idea pages, 120
  observed activities, 131
Toddler behavior
  idea pages, 120
  observed activities, 130
Toddler care
  idea pages, 120
  observed activities, 129
Toddlers, infants and. See Infants and toddlers
Toys
  infants, for, 120, 128
  toddlers, for, 120, 133
Transition strategies, early childhood
  idea pages, 136
  observed activities, 140
Transition strategies, elementary
  idea pages, 136
  observed activities, 146

U

Units, 101

V

Videography, 223, 230
Visitors, music and movement, 13
Volunteers, parents as
  idea pages, 176
  observed activities, 183

W

Walking in the halls, 147
Water play, outdoor
  idea pages, 92
  observed activities, 97
Water tables
  idea pages, 48
  materials used in, 50
Webbing pages, 101
Web sites, recommended, 162, 175
Whole-group cooking ideas
  idea pages, 64
  observed activities, 67–68
Word games, 23
Word-wall ideas, 31
Working with children with special needs, 151–161
  ideas, 151
Working with parents, 176–183
  ideas, 176
Writing activities
  fine motor development, activities for, 94
  idea pages, 23
  observed activities, 32